POST-KEYNESIAN ECONOMIC THEORY

RECENT ECONOMIC THOUGHT SERIES

Editors:

Warren J. Samuels
Michigan State University
East Lansing, Michigan, USA

William Darity, Jr.
University of North Carolina
Chapel Hill, North Carolina, USA

Other books in the series:

Mercuro, N.: TAKING PROPERTY AND JUST COMPENSATION
de Marchi, N.: POST-POPPERIAN METHODOLOGY OF ECONOMICS
Gapinski, J.: THE ECONOMICS OF SAVING
Darity, W.: LABOR ECONOMICS: PROBLEMS IN ANALYZING LABOR MARKETS
Caldwell, B. and Boehm, S.: AUSTRIAN ECONOMICS: TENSIONS AND DIRECTIONS
Tool, Marc R.: INSTITUTIONAL ECONOMICS: THEORY, METHOD, POLICY
Babe, Robert E.: INFORMATION AND COMMUNICATION IN ECONOMICS
Magnusson, Lars: MERCANTILIST ECONOMICS
Garston, Neil: BUREAUCRACY: THREE PARADIGMS
Friedman, James W.: PROBLEMS OF COORDINATION IN ECONOMIC ACTIVITY
Magnusson, Lars: EVOLUTIONARY AND NEO-SCHUMPETERIAN APPROACHES TO ECONOMICS
Reisman, D.: ECONOMIC THOUGHT AND POLITICAL THEORY
Burley, P. and Foster, J.: ECONOMICS AND THERMODYNAMICS: NEW PERSPECTIVES ON ECONOMIC ANALYSIS
Brennan, H.G. and Waterman, A.C.: ECONOMICS AND RELIGION: ARE THEY DISTINCT?
Klein, Philip A.: THE ROLE OF ECONOMIC THEORY
Semmler, Willi.: BUSINESS CYCLES: THEORY AND EMPIRICS
Little, Daniel: ON THE RELIABILITY OF ECOONOMIC MODELS: ESSAYS IN THE PHILOSOPHY OF ECONOMICS
Weimer, David L.: INSTITUTIONAL DESIGN
Davis, John B.: THE STATE OF THE INTERPRETATION OF KEYNES

POST-KEYNESIAN ECONOMIC THEORY

Edited by

Paul Wells
University of Illinois @ Urbana-Champaign
Champaign, IL 61820

Springer Science+Business Media, LLC

Library of Congress Cataloging-in-Publication Data

Post-Keynesian economic theory / edited by Paul Wells.
p. cm. -- (Recent economic thought series)
Includes bibliographical references and index.
ISBN 978-1-4613-5987-6 ISBN 978-1-4615-2331-4 (eBook)
DOI 10.1007/978-1-4615-2331-4
1. Keynesian economics. I. Wells, Paul J., 1925-
II. Series
HB99.7.P68 1995
330.15'6--dc20 95-8144
CIP

Originally published by Kluwer Academic Publishers in 1995
Softcover reprint of the hardcover 1st edition 1995

Printed on acid-free paper.

CONTENTS

PREFACE

I first suggested to Paul Wells that he should edit a volume for this series in early 1989. His proposal for the collection, which I obviously supported, indicated two objectives: to add significantly to our understanding of the economic behavior of capitalist systems and to provide an assessment of the status, limitations, and opportunities for further significant research, the second of which made the volume suitable for this series. It has been my experience that the pursuit of the general objective of this series—for each volume to provide an assessment of the present status, problems, and prospects for its respective field—could be operationalized and accomplished in various ways. Wells's proposal seemed congruent and so it has proven to be.

Alas, well into the process of assembling this collection Paul developed a serious illness and was unable either to further edit the volume or to prepare an introduction. This accounts for my writing this preface—my only contribution other than recruiting Wells. I am very much aware that Paul would have very likely produced a significantly different introduction—for example, stressing or expanding on different ideas and themes. All praise is due Janet R. Fitch of the Office of Research, College of Commerce and Business Administration, University of Illinois at Urbana–Champaign, for her efforts in seeing this volume through to publication on Paul's behalf.

For the reader not entirely, if at all, conversant with Post-Keynesian (with or without the hyphen) economics, it may be useful to advert to a letter that Paul wrote to me in October 1989. He referred to the importance of the matter of determinate solutions for understanding the difference between neoclassical and Keynes's economics (referring to Samuels, 1989; see also Samuels, 1991). The matter of determinacy is indeed significant and for several reasons.

The quest for determinate solutions has several sources. One is the psychological desire or need for certitude (if not certainty), simplicity, coherence, and closure in human affairs, especially in a world that is arguably, in important if not all major respects, of human construction. A second involves the belief that the consummation of an intellectual discipline requires the reaching of singular, unique, and determinate solutions to analytical problems. Third is the related belief that policy advice, if it is to be taken seriously, must be predicated on singular, unique, determinate solutions.

One significance of these operative considerations has been the making of severely limiting methodological and substantive assumptions to permit the economic theorist and policy analyst to generate unique determinate solutions. The world portrayed in such work is hypothetical or imaginary, conjectural, and artificial—even illusory, albeit often beguiling—and, in a very real sense, a matter of economic science fiction. It is useful but still not economic reality; in short, it is what Ronald Coase refers to, with disdain, as "blackboard economics."

Mainstream microeconomics and macroeconomics have been conducted with the objective of reaching unique determinate solutions and facilitating them with the use of analytical techniques. Thus, for example, the standard "Keynesian cross" is used to reach unique determinate equilibrium incomes, thereby obscuring the existence of the wide range of different types of variables actually at work in the economy.

This brings me to a second respect in which the matter of determinacy is significant: to wit, its use in conjunction with equilibrium modelling. Equilibrium analysis is a useful device permitting the analysis of the consequences of more or less marginal changes in causal variables. But at least three problems characterize conventional equilibrium analysis. One is, again, the need to make limiting methodological and substantive assumptions to permit the economic theorist and policy analyst to generate unique, determinate *equilibrium* solutions, thereby ruling certain variables out of analytical bounds and consideration. A second is that the real world is never in equilibrium; it is always awash in a multiplicity of disequilibrating and equilibrating movements; equilibrium is an analytical fiction or tool. Third, the combination of both of the foregoing and the conventional focus on identifying the technical conditions of existence and stability of equilibrium—often using elegant and otherwise impressive abstract mathematical tools—has tended to eclipse and diminish the importance of the factors and forces and the processes of adjustment actually at work in the economy.

One source of the resulting mechanistic treatment of the economy is the incipient belief in an independently given and operating "natural" economy, a real world of markets and prices independent of human institutions and actions. One related, historically conventional practice has been to assume the neutrality of money—namely, that monetary institutions (including commercial and central banks) and variables (including the demand and supply of money, interest rates, and price level) have no effect on the level and composition of output or have effect only during unusual, perhaps aberrational, times. The effect is to define the economy as independent of money and monetary and financial institutions and variables.

The foregoing is presently significant because the essays comprising this collection, entirely commissioned by Paul Wells, differ from such mainstream practice. For one thing, their authors do not seek unique, determinate results or models that would produce them. Second, their authors do not treat money and monetary variables as neutral. More realistically and more interestingly, the authors explore, first, the multiplicity of macromonetary variables actually at work in the economy and, second, the operation of "the economy" as it actually exists within the regime of, and specific to, particular institutions and groups of institutions, including monetary and financial institutions.

Thus, in the essay by Sheila Dow one finds attention to the impact of real-world financial institutions, behavioral practices, and circumstances on liquidity preference, a key variable in the determination of national (and world) income. Her analysis relates most directly, but by no means solely, to the Post-Keynesian theory of the firm and corporate finance and to international finance markets. It is conducted, moreover, in a matter that distinguishes between the different conditions or circumstances characterizing (1) center-periphery, (2) level of economic development, and (3) international borrowing and lending by developing countries. Liquidity preference is shown to be not a simple, and certainly not a given and singular, phenomenon. Moreover, it is relevant always, not simply in cases of capital flight, though, as she points out, this is a practice worthy of specific attention. The consequences of the institutions, behavioral practices, and circumstances that pertain to liquidity preference are real, in the usual sense of that term in monetary and macroeconomic theory (as distinguished from philosophical or scientific realism). She may be correct in also arguing that monetary factors are, if anything, more significant for the lowest-income developing countries. Be that as it may, she certainly establishes the argument for their importance in all cases, which implies the *pro tanto* poverty of any analysis which excludes them.

Dow's analysis is complemented by that of Fernando J. Cardim de Carvalho. It, too, deals with liquidity preference theory but for the most part explores quite different aspects. Both authors, of course, deal with a monetary economy—specifically, with a monetary theory of production, which cannot meaningfully and completely be analyzed and understood through models that effectively assume a barter economy. De Carvalho's survey and assessment covers liquidity preference as a theory of money demand; a theory of general asset pricing; and a theory of money supply; as well as a theory of money under the conditions of permanent and high inflation, which is also, in a way, a theory of the dynamics of inflationary processes. In this article as well as Dow's, money's nonneutrality is comprehended in part through understanding the important endogenous origins of the supply of money, which is tantamount to emphasizing the creative role of banks in providing money in the form of credit.

The contribution by Nina Shapiro and Tracy Mott transfers attention to a field in which Post-Keynesians ply their quite different approach to economics, the theory of the firm, and its pricing. Their analysis focuses on the expectations and enterprise decisions involved in mark-up pricing in markets in which competitive demand and supply does not, in the view of Post-Keynesians, adequately describe and explain economic operation and performance. Shapiro and Mott identify the differences between, and the different circumstances to which apply, the mark-up price models of Michal Kalecki, Joseph Steindl, and Alfred Eichner. Consideration of the diverse forms that market power can take pervades their discussion. Although their explicit foci are on the degree of monopoly; growth and survival under conditions of market power, including market development; and the role of strategic pricing, a continuing theme is the importance within the firm of working out the meaning of profit maximization. The richness of economic possibilities—in contrast with the artificial provision of presumptive, unique determinate solutions on the basis of substantively limiting assumptions—is underscored by their emphasis on differences of market structure and of corporate strategies as well as by their noting, in the concluding paragraph, that all this is true in addition to the fact of variability of such Keynesian variables as the propensity to save and the marginal efficiency of capital.

Douglas Vickers's contribution represents, in effect, a combination of the liquidity interests of the Dow and de Carvalho essays and the theory of the firm of the Shapiro and Mott essay. But his contribution also has intended significance for the nonneutrality of money in the actual economy. One way to approach this essay is to appreciate that firms and households make decisions not solely with regard to real variables but in the context and on the basis of expectations (uncertainty and ignorance, in the sense of George Shackle) and differential access to capital and money markets, which implies important real consequences of the operation of banks. These are among the variables governing the level of economic activity—the level of real income in the GNP or any other sense. *Capital* remains plant and equipment, but the formation, disposition, and use of *money capital* is a vital part of the actual economic process, as is, therefore, also the operation of the financial system, including but not limited to commercial banks. Liquidity *qua* liquidity considerations are considered a not insubstantial part of these processes. Still, much more is involved, including variations in the level and structure of production consequent to (changes in) who can generate and who can acquire money capital and, in each case, under what conditions.

Vickers surveys a sample of the relevant historical classical-neoclassical literature, as well as the modern literature, especially that relating to neutrality versus nonneutrality of money. Vickers's coverage is so wide ranging that the objective and open-minded reader must finally ask: Given the variety of substantive topics seen to be pertinent to the question, how could the nonneutrality of money be taken as anything but the result of an ideologically or artificially driven set of assumptions? Either these monetary-macroeconomic topics are irrelevant which clearly they are not or, if relevant, they must materially affect the level and composition of output. Money is clearly both endogenous, at least in part, and nonneutral. Money matters, and corporate and personal finance matters.

In the next essay, William Darity, Jr., who has, since the present collection was arranged, become co-editor of this series, and Arthur H. Goldsmith examine the concepts of "natural rate of unemployment" and "full employment." Basically, their argument is that it is arbitrary and fundamentally unenlightening, in a world of multiple variables, to construct critically important definitions solely in terms of one variable or one relationship. Any straight-forward link, for example, between labor market clearing and full employment, is rendered untenable because of further complexities introduced by such other variables as the relationship between real and money wages, unemployment exposure, real asset values, interest rates, individual utility behavior, liquidity preference, search unemployment, money illusion, efficiency wages, and, *inter alia*, definitions of voluntary and involuntary unemployment. Standard practice, which seeks single-valued numbers for one or another conception of unemployment rates, thus is shown to be myopic because it conflicts with two other, richer insights of economics: first, that all variables are interdependent; and second, that relationships are not single-valued but are functional—for example, in the representation of commodity demand as generally having some degree of price or income elasticity.

Darity and Goldsmith also closely examine the history of the concepts of full employment and the natural rate of unemployment, the treatments (such as they were) prior to Keynes, by Keynes, and since Keynes, especially that of so-called New Keynesian (different from Post-Keynesian) economics. They conclude in a manner akin to Keynes dictum on the natural rate of interest—namely, that it is neither useful nor significant for analysis.

The essay by Edward J. Amadeo raises other issues. It is consistent with the general theme concerning unduly limiting methodological and substantive assumptions. Amadeo critiques conventional belief and practice by arguing that instability can arise even in the absence of time and money (money as a numeraire and only a medium of exchange) because of uncertainty due to atomized and uncoordinated decentralized decision-making. He, too, emphasizes the role of liquidity in complicating the generation of aggregate economic performance and reinforcing the reasoning leading to the conclusion that the institution of money is not neutral. Demand for money for purposes of liquidity (as an argument in actors' utility functions) means both that money is more than a medium of exchange and that changes in liquidity preference affect output of ordinary commodities.

Amadeo also has important things to say about the set of ideas and theories that relates real/money wage rates to equilibrium and unemployment. Here, he evaluates both what Keynes had to say and what Keynes, or Keynes's theory, has been understood to say—arguably two quite different things. Amadeo also raises some points congruent with the essay by Darity and Goldsmith. He is not the first to argue that the reception, understanding, and development of Keynes's ideas was fundamentally governed by ideological considerations, often unconscious but nonetheless effective. Amadeo properly makes much of the fact that contrary to Keynes's own theory, much of the profession ascribes to him the view that unemployment is a function of money wage rigidity. But this, too, Amadeo suggests, is a function of the proclivity of orthodox economists to produce harmonistic models congruent with the unmitigated optimistic affirmation of market economies.

In sum, this collection represents a constructive Post-Keynesian critique of contemporary macroeconomic conceptualization and practice. It clearly demonstrates the richness and, therefore, the complexity and the inexorable difficulties of doing meaningful macroeconomic theory. It also demonstrates the illusory character of seeking unique determinate results to problems of macroeconomics.

I am confident that the contributors join me in dedicating this volume to

Paul Wells, its vibrant, thoughtful, and heterodox editor. One can only hope that it is a fitting tribute to his career of scholarship.

WARREN J. SAMUELS

REFERENCES

Samuels, Warren J. (1989). "Determinate Solutions and Valuational Processes: Overcoming the Foreclosure of Process." *Journal of Post Keynesian Economics*, 11 (Summer), 531–546.

———. (1991). "Determinate Solutions and the Foreclosure of Process: A Response to Garretsen," *Journal of Post Keynesian Economics*, 13 (Spring), 424–430.

POST-KEYNESIAN ECONOMIC THEORY

1

LIQUIDITY PREFERENCE IN INTERNATIONAL FINANCE: THE CASE OF DEVELOPING COUNTRIES

SHEILA C. DOW

1.1. INTRODUCTION

Keynes's monetary theory is based on the view that money is fundamentally nonneutral. Money is an institution integral to the capitalist process, and monetary developments are part of the process that determines output and employment. Keynes's theory has been developed to apply to modern conditions by Post-Keynesian monetary theory (see Davidson, 1972; Minsky, 1985; and Wray, 1990).

According to this theory, the supply of money is determined significantly by the banking system (albeit influenced by the monetary authorities). The banking system supplies credit according to its state of liquidity preference, while borrowers demand credit according to their liquidity preference; *liquidity preference* is here being interpreted broadly to refer to the portfolio choices of banks and financial borrowers and the choices of nonfinancial firms with respect to purchasing capital goods and the form of financing this purchase. Liquidity preference is thus determined by the state of confidence in the prices of the full range of assets, financial and nonfinancial. Shifting liquidity preference influences the supply of and demand for credit, as well as output and employment.

It is the purpose of this chapter to explore this representation of Post-Keynesian monetary theory in an international context. In general terms, if money is nonneutral internationally, then international monetary developments can have real international consequences. In addition to the general question of nonneutrality, the international dimension poses further questions (parallel to those in regional economics) about the implications of financial integration among different economies. In other words, if money is nonneutral, is its effect on output and employment different in different types of economy, and how is this affected by different international institutional arrangements? There are two contexts in which this discussion has particular relevance. The first is the European Monetary Union, where a series of measures is planned to ensure financial integration; this is discussed in terms of Post-Keynesian monetary theory in Chick (1991) and Dow (1994). Here the focus rather will be on the other context of developing countries and international financial markets.

In the next section, Post-Keynesian monetary theory is outlined in more detail with a general formulation in the international context. The following sections outline the case of developing countries with respect to international financial markets. First their situation is couched in terms of center-periphery analysis and then in terms of credit demand and availability, and finally capital flight is analyzed in terms of liquidity preference theory. Reference is made to the Bank for International Settlements (BIS) data on international borrowing and lending. The international liquid assets of developing countries will be considered alongside their borrowing; the liquid portfolio position of many low-income developing countries can be seen to reflect not only credit availability constraints but also a high degree of liquidity preference, which discourages the demand for credit.

1.2. Post-Keynesian Monetary Theory in an International Context

Quite apart from the logical and doctrinal shortcomings of such a polarization (see Dow and Dow, 1989), neither approach adapts well to the international context. In the context of a partial analysis of a closed economy, it could be argued either that the domestic money supply may be taken as given or that the demand for credit is fully accommodated. But in an open economy context it is hard to justify abstraction from the fact that international credit flows not only endogenize the supply of credit, but also from the fact that there are availability constraints on the supply of credit in international markets. Given that the amount of international borrowing and lending and the choice of instruments employed reflects the choice of to how much liquidity to preserve or to forgo, it seems clear that a Post-

Keynesian international monetary theory must incorporate both the liquidity preference and endogenous money strands.

Minsky's (1982) analysis of financial fragility provides an excellent basis for the analysis to be developed here. Minsky's (1975) theory of investment combines Keynes's concept of animal spirits with a theory of firms' financial behavior. The volume of investment is determined jointly by the expected value of the assets to be purchased, the availability of internal funds, the willingness to incur debt, and the willingness of financial institutions to supply debt. The willingness to incur debt depends on the firm's perception of borrower's risk while the willingness of financial institutions to supply debt depends on their perception of lender's risk. The demand for and supply of credit are, thus, inextricably tied up with the liquidity preference of the parties concerned. The more confident firms are in the returns expected from the investment, the more willing they are to adopt a highly geared financial structure. The more confident lenders are in the expected returns and, thus, in the likelihood of principle and interest being repaid, the greater the availability of credit. Credit creation is thus endogenous but, not, in general, fully accommodating; credit demand, in turn, in general is also constrained by liquidity preference.

This analysis can be generalized to apply to financial institutions' own borrowing with their own creditors assessing the risk of default on the part of the borrowing financial institutions (see Dow and Earl, 1982, ch. 11). Taken in conjunction with the borrowing financial institution's assessment of the expected value of its own assets, we have the makings of a general theory of financial behavior. If, further, the analysis of firms' investment behavior is adapted to the borrowing of sovereign governments to finance development projects, with domestic revenues being substituted for retained earnings, the theory can be applied directly to the situation of developing countries' exposure to international financial markets.

Before proceeding to consider whether there are likely to be any systemic patterns to the situation of developing countries in international financial markets, there is a central element of Minsky's financial fragility hypothesis that may have particular application to this context. The theory of investment itself does not address the question of the time profile of earnings and payments; the focus is on how much is borrowed and at what price and on the consequences of expectations not being met (default if earnings are insufficient to repay the debt). The system is then more fragile as the structure of finance is more highly geared and, thus, is more vulnerable to defaults being spread through the system from borrower to lender, causing an escalation of defaults.

But the fragility of the financial system is increased further if the earnings stream is seriously out of line with interest payments and the requirement to repay principle—that is, if there are cash-flow problems. Minsky (1982, ch. 5) outlines a progression from conservative hedge finance, whereby the earnings stream is sufficient to cover interest payments; to speculative finance, where it is confidently expected that refinancing will be available if necessary to meet interest payments; to Ponzi finance, where there is no expectation of refinancing and all hinges on high expected returns to the assets purchased. The choice of a particular form of finance is an indication of liquidity preference, with hedge financiers having the highest liquidity preference. But borrowers can find themselves moving involuntarily along the spectrum as a result of changes in interest charges and changes in the availability of credit for refinancing. Thus, an increased perception of borrower's risk will both raise interest rates and reduce credit availability, pushing hedge financiers into speculative finance and even Ponzi finance. As a result, the fragility of the system is increased as well as the risk of default, which multiplies in a fragile financial environment. In what follows, therefore, it will be important to note that actual borrowing and lending and their relationship to real economic conditions reflect the interdependent factors of choice and constraints on choice.

1.3. Developing Countries in a Center-Periphery Framework

In order to construct a hypothesis as to the relationship between developing countries and international capital markets, we need to consider the characteristics conventionally associated with developing economies. These characteristics can be summarized in the following stylized facts:

- A relative reliance on primary production;
- A relatively high degree of openness, with exports predominantly primary products and low-level manufactured goods;
- Relatively volatile export receipts and deteriorating terms of trade over time;
- A relatively high degree of foreign ownership;
- Low per capita wealth; and
- Low per capita income.

These characteristics have been shown to be interdependent by dependency theory, which explains the pattern of production, trade, and investment, and the persistently low levels of per capita income as the outcome of the dependence of emerging economies on the markets, finance, and technology of developed economies (see Frank, 1978; Seers, 1981). The pattern of borrowing and lending suggested by this framework is as follows: when export markets are buoyant, the expected return on investment will be high, and there will be large inflows of capital in the form of direct investment. But the volatile nature of export receipts makes the return on investment, and thus capital inflows, volatile. At times of export shortfall and withdrawal of inward investment, there will be an urgent need for borrowing to finance the balance of payments deficit; if funds are not available from international capital markets (in the form of new borrowing or liquidation of existing assets), then recourse must be made to downward income adjustment to reduce absorption, reinforcing the low levels of per capita income.

Not all developing economies fall easily into this framework. Those that do may be classified as low-income developing countries. But there are other categories. There are the oil-producing developing countries, most of which have acquired sufficient wealth during periods of high export receipts to reduce their dependency on foreign capital and to achieve high levels of per capita income. There are the newly industrialized countries (NICs), which have successfully broken through into export markets in manufactured goods and have, thereby, achieved financial independence and increased levels of per capita income. And finally there are what are termed the middle-income countries, which lie somewhere between the NICs and the low-income developing countries.

For all of these categories, cumulative causation theory can add a further dimension to dependency theory. According to this theory, introduced by Myrdal (1963), productivity advantage is cumulative; it is therefore extremely difficult for latecomers to particular forms of production to compete successfully with established producers. The low wealth levels of emerging countries contributes to this productivity disadvantage because balance-of-payments problems are more likely to require income adjustment, since a cushion of foreign financial assets is not available. Since the financial sector of developed countries likewise enjoys productivity advantages, it is difficult for emerging economies to develop an indigenous financial sector that can compete internationally.

The development-inhibiting effects of productivity disadvantage are termed *backwash effects*. But Myrdal (1963) pointed out that there are countervailing spread effects, whereby the emerging economies can benefit from the developed economies: markets for exports, technology transfer, a stock of wealth that can finance investment in emerging economies, and a sophisticated financial system that can create credit to finance investment and provide a high return on domestic savings allocated to it. For countries in the three categories (oil producers, NICs, and middle-income economies), the spread effects have to a greater or lesser degree outweighed the backwash effects. These economies, therefore, are unlikely to be any more constrained in their access to international capital markets than developed economies.

But with the exception of those NICs that have developed indigenous financial markets on a par with those in developed economies (notably Hong Kong), there remains the fact of the differential in sophistication between internal and external financial markets. This issue has not been addressed directly either by dependency theory or by cumulative causation theory. However, Chick's (1986) evolution of banking framework has been applied to dependency theory, with elements of cumulative causation theory, by Chick and Dow (1988). The evolution of banking framework analyzes the historical development of banking systems in terms of the scope of the banking system to create credit and the way in which the causal process changes with the institutional and economic environment.

At their current stage of evolution, banks in developed countries have achieved considerable independence in their capacity to create credit; the constraint is much more one of capital base than of reserves, which the central bank undertakes to supply on demand. In their search for increased market share, banks seek to lend and seek deposits to finance the loans. As long as the market supports this activity by reinforcing the banks' capital base, banks are free to expand credit; but there is an upward bias in interest rates, as banks compete for deposits. Borrowers must, therefore, require adequate returns on investment to pay the correspondingly high rate on loans. Lending tends to be concentrated more toward firms with market power and speculative investment, both of which may offer higher returns.

In developing economies, however, the banking system is at an earlier stage of evolution, with banks much more constrained in their credit-creating activities. For example, the logistics of clearing in countries with poor communications are such that fine-tuning bank portfolios is very difficult. Further, the interbank market may be undeveloped, so that each bank is closely constrained by its own reserves. Currently developed countries, when at a similar stage of banking evolution, proceeded through the subsequent stages of banking development in response to market pressure. But the financial needs of currently developing countries can, in part, be met already through international capital markets. Not only may this inhibit the evolution of the indigenous banking system, but it also influences the character of borrowing and lending.

Referring back to Minsky's model outlined earlier, bank finance is made available according to the risk assessment by the banks of the potential borrowers. This assessment in turn depends on information. In general, information is poorer when the borrower is more remote (physically or culturally); further, the costs of acquiring information are higher with a lower initial information base and a smaller the borrower. Just as small firms in remote regions in a developed country experience a credit gap, so one might expect a credit gap to exist in developing countries for local borrowers on which the bank has poor information. This information gap may be overcome by a strong sense of optimism among banks coupled with a lack of alternative borrowers. But the basis for optimism is fragile if based on poor information, and the risk assessment is liable to sudden reversals. The situation is also fragile with respect to interest charges. International borrowing, which was conservative initially, may become speculative or Ponzi finance if interest rates rise relative to earnings. This is true regardless of how good the information was on which the lending decision was based.

Finally, consideration must be given to the propensity of developing countries to borrow and to hold assets liquid. Liquidity preference is higher when there is less confidence in the value of nonliquid assets. Given the long experience of economic vulnerability in developing economies, liquidity preference is likely to be high. Thus, despite the high opportunity cost in terms of development opportunities foregone, there will be a tendency for governments to hold assets liquid as a cushion against balance-of-payments crises for which external finance may not be available. Local entrepreneurs, too, will be vulnerable to unpredicted shortages of foreign exchange with which to service debt. The preference will be for liquid assets in the form of deposits with foreign banks, rather than domestic banks, since the assets of the domestic banks will be among those in which confidence is muted. The productivity advantage then of foreign banks will have the spread effect of providing liquidity, but the backwash effect of encouraging capital outflows and impeding the development of the local banking system. In considering in the next section the actual borrowing and lending experience of developing countries, therefore, it must be borne in mind that borrowing may be constrained not only by the adverse assessment by banks, but also by the low confidence that discourages the demand for credit, on the part of both governments and local entrepreneurs.

1.4. International Borrowing and Lending by Developing Countries

The debt crisis is generally explained by an overexpansion of bank lending to developing countries in the 1970s as a result of the combination of an underassessment of country risk by the banks and an oversupply of funds due to weak credit demand in the less risky developed countries. In Minskian-plus-dependency-theory terms, the crisis can be explained rather differently as increasing fragility caused by increased interest rates in conjunction with reduced export earnings produced by weakening demand in developed countries and high import payments due to high oil prices (see Helleiner, 1990, and Loxley, 1986, for two excellent accounts). The refinancing to avert default simply added to the fragility of the borrowers' financing and exacerbated the risk of default. The only outlet was depression of domestic demand to dampen imports.

But implicit in these characterizations is the assumption that developing countries generally have an excess demand for credit, which is supplied when alternative borrowers do not come forward. This interpretation suffers from two shortcomings. First, it is often expressed in loanable funds terms: given global saving, there is a certain amount of credit available that can be distributed among borrowers. From the perspective of the Chick framework, rather, banks can create as much credit as the market will bear (in the form of the banks' capital base). The expansion of credit to developing countries can then be seen as the result of the market-supporting banks in their wish to promote market share and expansion by building up developing-country business. When the financial structure of developing economies became more fragile due at least in part to external developments, the banks reassessed the profitability of these loans, raised interest charges, and reduced availability. This is currently being reinforced by a reduced market tolerance for continued bank lending in a fragile environment; there has been a considerable lag between the fragility creating a debt crisis and the market valuation of bank assets being adjusted.

Second, the interpretation outlined above does not make explicit the role of liquidity preference. For particularly vulnerable economies, it is too risky to seek loans. This is the case for governments, which risk having to impose unpopular balance-of-payments adjustment policies, and for local entrepreneurs, who risk bankruptcy if their asset base is low, in the event of low foreign-exchange gains with which to repay loans. Rather, there will be lending to international capital markets as a means of maintaining some minimal level of liquidity. Without liquidity preference, one would expect a long-term pattern of most developing countries being significant net borrowers from international capital markets, with the degree of borrowing depending on the variations in banks' risk assessment. With liquidity preference, one would expect the more vulnerable developing economies to be net lenders to foreign banks.

The Bank for International Settlements publishes data on international borrowing and lending by commercial banks, which allows some assessment of the hypothesis outlined earlier. Table 1.1 sets out data over a ten-year period (1982–1991) by groupings of countries according to

TABLE 1.1. THE RATIO BETWEEN DEPOSITS WITH AND BORROWINGS FROM INTERNATIONAL BANKS, 1982–1991 MARCH 1991 (IN PERCENTAGES)

Year	Inside Area	Outside Dev'ed	Eastern Europe	OPEC	Other Latin America	Other Middle East	Other Africa	Other Asia
1982	111.5	49.2	20.4	212.8	24.3	171.5	55.4	70.4
1983[a]	109.9	41.7	31.8	161.3	21.6	169.5	48.0	75.2
1984	110.3	31.6	41.1	128.2	27.8	134.6	46.5	82.1
1985	110.6	32.2	40.5	139.7	32.1	130.7	54.5	84.0
1986	110.5	33.9	42.6	141.2	32.2	133.7	53.9	78.1
1987	106.8	41.5	37.9	119.6	31.2	134.2	55.3	91.3
1988	105.6	44.7	37.1	135.7	36.5	152.0	65.6	93.0
1989	105.5	54.2	39.1	143.5	38.8	165.3	76.2	94.9
1990	101.6	73.1	33.4	164.5	55.5	237.0	98.7	118.9
1991	100.4	71.3	20.6	182.1	64.1	294.1	110.7	111.7

Source: BIS, *International Banking and Financial Market Developments* (various issues).

[a]Change in data coverage (see January 1986, Table 4).

whether they are developed and inside or outside the BIS reporting area (or, in effect, by high or low per capita income, respectively), OPEC, or developing, by geographical area. The statistic selected to indicate degree of liquidity preference is the ratio between total deposits with international banks and total borrowing. The ratio is higher when the liquidity preference is higher, both as regards desire to hold assets liquid and as regards the unwillingness to incur debt; the ratio may also reflect the presence of credit rationing, an expression of the banks' liquidity preference with respect to potential borrowers. This ratio has been calculated on the basis of the aggregate deposits and borrowings of each grouping.

From this table it is apparent that, while some developing countries have been significant net borrowers from the international banking system, others have been significant net lenders. Borrowing and lending by the major developed countries has been roughly balanced over the period. But other developed countries and Eastern Europe have been significant net borrowers, although their deposits are still a higher proportion of borrowing than the Latin American countries. Non-OPEC Africa and Asia in aggregate have, however, maintained deposits as a higher proportion of borrowing than any of these three groups, and their aggregate deposits now exceed their borrowing. For these countries, the opportunity cost both of holding sizeable deposits and not borrowing is very high; it can only be explained by a combination of high liquidity preference and credit rationing by the banks.

Aggregate data, of course, gloss over wide disparities in individual countries' experience and behavior. Table 1.2 presents the same liquidity preference measure as Table 1.1 but disaggregates by per capita income class. The median ratio is shown for each income grouping, as classified by the World Bank, ordered by per capita income, subdivided into tertiles. The ratios are shown for outstanding balances of deposits and loans in June 1991.

These data suggest a pattern of high liquidity preference for the poorest countries, possibly in conjunction with limitations on credit availability. The ratio falls steadily until the higher-income middle-income countries, after which it moves erratically. For higher-income countries without credit constraints, borrowing and lending would not be expected to follow any particular pattern by income class. Clearly, much more investigation is

TABLE 1.2. MEDIAN RATIO OF INTERNATIONAL BANK DEPOSITS TO BANK LOANS BY PER CAPITA INCOME, JUNE 1991 (IN PERCENTAGES)

	Country Groupings,[a] Tertiles			
	Low-Income	Middle Income	Lower-Middle Income	Upper-High Income
I	207.0	99.9	37.6	81.2
II	316.5	94.6	92.8	114.9
III	131.9	72.2	100.8	60.9

Sources: World Bank, *World Development Report* (1991, Table 1, p. 204).
BIS, *International Banking and Financial Market Developments* (November 1991, Table 5A).
[a]Based on 1989 GNP per capita, World Bank definitions.

warranted of the conditions underlying these data. But this limited evidence does lend support to the proposition that the lowest-income countries may well be credit constrained but are also constrained by the need to maintain their limited assets in liquid form. The standard picture of developing countries having taken advantage of a period of ready access to international credit applies only to the higher-income developing countries.

A preliminary inspection of the pre-1982 data suggests that the liquidity ratio was, in fact, even higher for low-income developing countries in this period. Given the more liberal lending behavior of the banks at that time, this suggests that the demand for credit was not forthcoming. The relatively higher level of assets held with the international banks presumably reflected the more favorable international economic climate and terms of trade of the time. In other words, at a time when credit availability and foreign-exchange earnings were less constrained than in 1991, low-income countries appear to have expressed and satisfied a relatively high liquidity preference.

1.5. Capital Flight

Attention has been drawn to the assets of some developing countries held in international capital markets, as an indicator of capital flight. Concern has been expressed at the possibility that capital flight has exacerbated the debt crisis (see, for example, Lessard and Williamson, 1987). The concept of capital flight is intended to capture the possibility of private-sector capital outflows from developing countries that make it even more difficult for central banks of heavily indebted countries to meet their foreign-exchange commitments.

The concept of capital flight is generally intended to refer only to those capital outflows responding to "undue" domestic risk: of devaluation, of financial repression, or of taxation to fund debt. It is often envisaged as a wave-like phenomenon, as perceptions of these risks fluctuate. The wave-like flows arise from a stock of domestic hot money, which on occasion seeks refuge in international financial markets. It is virtually impossible to distinguish capital flight from other sources of capital outflow. Further, the BIS data include public- as well as private-sector deposits. But the data outlined in the previous section give some indication of the scale of capital flight, in that even large debtors have substantial offsetting deposits. Using one technique for isolating capital flight from "normal outflows," the Bank of England (1989) estimates that the accumulated level of capital flight was over 30 percent of existing debt during 1981 through 1987.

The conventional explanations for capital flight rest predominantly on push factors—that is, features of domestic institutions and policy that are perceived as posing undue risk to domestic wealth holders. In that the problem of capital flight is seen in terms of exacerbation of the debt crisis, emphasis is placed on domestic policy to avert capital flight (see, for example, Lessard and Williamson, 1987). But Darity (1991) has explored more fully the pull factor of foreign banks encouraging capital flight. Rather than the traditional picture of banks passively accepting deposits and allocating them as loans, Darity presents the picture of banks as liability managers, seeking out high-profile borrowers and then the deposits to finance the loans. According to this interpretation, the same forces that encouraged the massive increase in developing-country bank borrowing in the 1970s also encouraged increased deposits with international banks. Darity pinpoints a direct interconnection between borrowing and lending by referring to the corruption entailed in applying the loans to unproductive purposes, the proceeds then being secreted in international financial markets.

The theoretical approach outlined in earlier sections suggests a more systemic force behind capital flight, still along the lines of pull factors. From the point of view of the lowest-income countries, large deposits with international banks involve a high opportunity cost. They constitute a problem in terms of these countries' development prospects just as much as does capital flight from countries with debt problems. Certainly the corruption thesis cannot be ruled out for these countries. Although they are not significant borrowers from private-sector banks, they are significant borrowers from the development agencies. However, the careful auditing procedures of international agencies significantly diminish the scope for corruption. But in addition, in the relative absence of market loans, the deposits are not connected to loans through liability management.

In fact, liability management does not require bank liabilities to have the same source as borrowing. The seeking for deposits induces capital outflows from all types of economies. The natural liquidity preference of the lowest-income developing countries is thus attracted to deposits with international banks. Chick (1986) classifies liability management as a feature of the fifth stage of banking development. Local banks in developing countries are at a much earlier stage of development. As a result, they are more constrained in their capacity to create credit. They are also unable to offer such attractive terms on deposits as international banks. As pointed out by Chick and Dow (1988), differential degrees of banking development between the center and the periphery encourage a redirection of banking business to center banks from periphery banks. This factor is reinforced by the fact that much of the earnings that find their way to international banks are held in the export enclave, often by branches of multinational concerns that already conduct their banking business with international rather than indigenous banks. Capital flight, or systematic capital outflows from low-income developing countries, is thus a natural result of liquidity preference in a center-periphery framework, rather than an aberration that can be corrected by marginal changes in domestic policy and institutions.

1.6. CONCLUSION

The question of the relationship between developing countries and the international banks was raised in the context of the neutrality or, otherwise, of money. The more familiar discussion of the debt crisis demonstrates the real consequences of monetary factors, in that massive restructuring programs have been introduced to generate the foreign exchange to meet debt commitments; these programs are addressed as much to deterring capital flight as to increasing foreign-exchange earnings on current account. Whether their consequences promote development or not, there is no doubt that the consequences are real.

Monetary factors are, if anything, more significant for the lowest-income developing countries. Credit availability for them is constrained by a low assessment by the banks of the monetary value of their collateral. But a long experience of economic and monetary vulnerability has also engendered a high liquidity preference in these countries. Given the large disparities in development of financial institutions between these countries and the international banking sector, liquidity preference is best satisfied by deposits in international banks. Given the foreign-exchange constraints on economic development, the opportunity cost of these deposits is very high.

The existence of a sophisticated international banking system provides a useful service in providing a haven for assets with a rate of return that reflects both high efficiency and the consequences of liability management. (The likelihood of relatively low risk attached to these deposits is less categorical given the potential fragility of the international financial system, but at least some spreading of risks is possible.) But increasing integration of financial markets world wide also carries dangers. First, there is the problem of the inhibition of the development of the indigenous banking system, an inhibition exacerbated by the tendency for domestic assets to be held in international capital markets. Even more important is the reliance on remote, large institutions for credit when it is demanded. (This dependency is reinforced if domestic financial development is stultified.) Assessment of the value of the assets of the lowest-income developing countries is bound to be based on limited information, causing these countries to experience problems of credit availability for reasons very similar to those experienced by small firms relative to large firms in developed countries.

The credit problems of developing countries are well documented, including those of the lowest-income countries. It has been my goal to show that these problems are consistent with a view of banks as unconstrained in the total of credit creation and as wielding power over the distribution of the credit they choose to create. Further, it has been shown that credit problems can be seen as part and parcel of the same forces behind liquidity preference: not only may banks choose not to create credit for reasons of liquidity preference, but the lowest-income countries may instead choose themselves to be net international lenders, for reasons of liquidity preference.

ACKNOWLEDGEMENT

I am grateful to Anne Thomson for comments.

REFERENCES

Bank of England. (1989). "Capital Flight." *Bank of England Quarterly Bulletin*, 364–367.

Chick, V. (1986). "The Evolution of the Banking System and the Theory of Saving, Investment and Interest." *Economies et Sociétés, Monnaie et Production*, 20, (3) 11–126.

———. (1991). "Some Scenarios for Money and Banking in the EC, and Their Regional Implications." University College London, mimeo.

Chick, V., and S. C. Dow. (1988). "A Post-Keynesian Perspective on Banking and Regional Development." In P. Arestis (Ed), *Post-Keynesian Monetary Economics*. Aldershot, U.K.: Elgar.

Darity, W., Jr. (1991). "Banking on Capital Flight." In P. Davidson and J. A. Kregel (Eds), *Economic Problems of the 1990s: Europe, the Developing Countries and the United States*. Aldershot, U.K.: Elgar.

Davidson, P. (1972). *Money and the Real World*. London: Macmillan.

Dow, A. C., and S. C. Dow. (1989). "Endogenous Money Creation and Idle Balances." In J. Pheby (Ed), *New Directions in Post-Keynesian Economics*, pp. 147–164. Aldershot, U.K.: Elgar.

Dow, S. C. (1994). "European Monetary Integration and the Distribution of Credit Availability." In S. Corbridge, R. Martin, and N. Thrift (Eds), *Money, Power and Space*. Oxford: Blackwell.

——— and P. E. Earl. (1982). *Money Matters: A Keynesian Approach to Monetary Economics*. Oxford: Martin Robertson.

Frank, A. G. (1978). *Dependent Accumulation and Underdevelopment*. London: Methuen.

Helleiner, G. K. (1990). *The New Global Economy and the Developing Countries*. Aldershot, U.K.: Elgar.

Kaldor, N. (1982). *The Scourge of Monetarism*. Oxford: Oxford University Press.

Lessard, D. R., and J. Williamson. (1987). *Capital Flight and Third World Debt*. Washington, DC: Institution for International Economics.

Loxley, J. (1986). *Debt and Disorder: External Financing for Development*. London: Westview.

Minsky, H. P. (1975). *John Maynard Keynes*. London: Macmillan.

———. (1982). *Can "It" Happen Again?* Armonk, NY: Sharpe. Also published as *Inflation, Recession and Economic Policy*. Brighton, U.K.: Wheatsheaf.

Myrdal, G. (1963). *Economic Theory and Underdeveloped Regions*. London: Methuen.

Seers, D. (1981). *Dependency Theory: A Critical Reassessment*. London: Frances Pinter.

Wray, L. R. (1990). *Money and Credit in Capitalist Economies: The Endogenous Money Approach*. Aldershot, U.K.: Elgar.

2

POST-KEYNESIAN DEVELOPMENTS OF LIQUIDITY PREFERENCE THEORY

FERNANDO J. CARDIM DE CARVALHO

2.1. INTRODUCTION

Post-Keynesian economics is a label that has included practically all kinds of non-Marxist criticisms of neoclassical economic theory. Keynesians, Kaleckians, Neo-Ricardians, Institutionalists and others have been identified, one time or another, as Post-Keynesians even though, in many senses, their mutual contrasts appear as large as those that opposed them to neoclassical economists. In this essay, however, I shall assign a much narrower meaning to the label. Here Post-Keynesian economics includes authors and researchers who consider Keynes's own attempts to build a new paradigm in economics, centered around the notion of monetary production economy, as the starting point for their own theoretical propositions.

In the preparation of *The General Theory* as well as in the debates that followed its publication, Keynes insisted that he was not offering an internal criticism of what he called classical economics. Rather, he was trying to convey the idea that the assumptions on which classical theory was based were inadequate to the analysis of a modern monetary economy. Classical theory was a paradigm centered on the analysis of a cooperative economy, something Minsky later aptly called a "village fair paradigm." According to Keynes, a monetary economy was not simply a complicated cooperative economy; it was something else, based on different rules and adapted to different ends. A whole new approach was necessary to understand it, not just an amendment, no matter how drastic, of orthodox economics.

This is not the place to develop in detail the concept of monetary economy,[1] but it is important to stress that the distinguishing feature of such an economy would be that in it, "money plays a part of its own and affects motives and decisions and is, in short, one of the operative factors in the situation, so that the course of events cannot be predicted, whether in the long period or in the short, without a knowledge of the behaviour of money between the first state and the last" (*CW*, XIII, pp. 408–409).

The long-period nonneutrality of money is the distinctive characteristic of a monetary economy. For money to be nonneutral in the long period, it has to leave permanent traces in the path the economy is expected to follow and in the state it is supposed to reach. Traditionally, long-period positions are established in terms of how the material world is shaped to satisfy social demands. Long-period nonneutrality of money means that the amount and structure of social wealth is affected by monetary forces. Money, in other words, has to affect how and how much capital is accumulated. It has to have a role in a theory of capital accumulation.[2]

Liquidity preference theory is based precisely on the perception that money can be more than just a means of circulation, oiling the economic machine, but can also become a form of wealth, an asset. The Post-Keynesian way to approach liquidity preference is, thus, to generalize it into a theory of asset choice and capital accumulation, along the lines set by Keynes in Chapter 17 of *The General Theory*. The behavior of money as an element of the stock of private wealth rather than merely a means of circulating the flow of income is the object of this school.

The origins of liquidity preference can be found in Keynes's earlier writings on the behavior of banks (see, for instance, *CW*, XIII, pp. 2–14) and the relation between banks and other financial institutions at the outbreak of World War I (*CW*, XI, ch. 4). In these essays Keynes showed how the increased uncertainty that surrounded financial operations in London when World War I began led banks and other institutions to substitute liquid for earning but illiquid assets in their portfolios, defeating the Bank of England's attempts to sustain prices of financial assets by increasing reserves. It was in the *Treatise on Money*, however, that the relation was made precise and generalized for agents other than banks. In the *Treatise*, money was proposed as an asset free of capital-uncertainty in contrast to bonds that had their prices subject to variations as the market rates of interest changed.[3] This theme was resumed in *The General Theory* in the form of a speculative motive for holding money instead of bonds. This source of demand for money, together with demand to satisfy precautionary and transactional motives, gave the best-known presentation of liquidity preference theory. Finally, in the post-publication debates with Ohlin around *The General Theory*, Keynes added a fourth motive, the finance motive, to demand money.

The neoclassical synthesis, beginning with Hicks's review articles on *The General Theory* and his 1939 book, *Value and Capital*, put Keynes's propositions on a different track than that emphasized here. Liquidity preference was reduced to a model of money demand in the narrow sense and evolved toward attempts to show that money demand could be sensitive to interest-rate changes even though uncertainty and liquidity premia were less and less referred to. Marshallian and Wicksellian strands of Keynesian theory were developed and Keynes's own themes, particularly his cogent discussion of the relation between money and nonprobabilistic uncertainty in his classic 1937 essay "The General Theory of Employment" (*CW*, XIV), never surfaced again in these models.

While the neoclassical synthesis was diluting liquidity preference, some authors, closer to Keynes, tried to develop his original insights. In 1951, Robinson (1979) extended his model of *the* interest rate for an explanation of the structure of interest rates. In 1954, Kahn (1972) besides presenting an alternative way to provide the same extension also reexamined Keynes's own treatment of the precautionary motive for holding money. Finally, in 1961 Shackle (1968), in a direct confrontation with neoclassical synthesis propositions, showed the inherent instability of equilibrium over time in asset markets, based as they are on divergent expectations.

The same issues were to be resumed by the already emerging Post-Keynesian school in the 1970s, with authors such as Davidson, Minsky, Wells, Weintraub and, later, Kregel, Chick, Dow and others. The premisses on which Keynes's model relies as well as its implications were rigorously described and examined. The instability of monetary and financial relations was described by Minsky. How these results were to be inserted into a larger macroeconomic theoretical model and, particularly, its relationship with the principle of effective demand and the notion of involuntary unemployment became a major concern of Post-Keynesian economics.

Post-Keynesian monetary theory has been a fast-growing industry since the late 1970s. This essay is not intended as a survey of the field but as a presentation of its main themes. In the following sections, I present the Post-Keynesian theory of liquidity preference in increasing degrees of generality.

Instead of an historical approach, showing how the concept evolved, I begin, in the second section, with a narrower presentation of liquidity preference as a theory of the behavior of the money market and the determination of the interest rate. In the third section, the model is generalized to many assets. The fourth section generalizes the model still further, showing that liquidity preference is not only a theory of money demand but also can be seen as a theory of money supply. The fifth section discusses changes in the established approach to money and liquidity in conditions of permanent and high inflation. Finally, the sixth section summarizes the main propositions of the essay.

2. 2. Money Demand

The cornerstone of Post-Keynesian monetary analysis is the relation between money and contracts. According to Keynes, the primary concept of money is money-of-account, the unit in which contracts are expressed (*CW*, V, p. 3). Money proper—that is, the thing which effectively circulates and discharges debts—represents the money-of-account. Again, according to Keynes, the moneyness of the legal tender, the thing that settles debts, is derived from its relation to the money-of-account and to contracts. Other assets that also play the role of money—namely of being accepted to liquidate contractual debts—derive their own moneyness from the possibility of replacing the legal tender under certain conditions.

Money becomes an asset precisely because of its capacity to discharge contractual debts when they come due (Davidson, 1978). This is the source of its liquidity. Forward money contracts project this property into the future. The more complete a system of forward contracts is, the safer an asset money becomes. When the time comes to settle debts, those who possess money do not run the risks of being incapable of honoring their commitments. Money becomes, thus, a general form of wealth, able to liquidate any kind of commitment, in contrast to other forms of wealth whose conversibility into means of payment is conditional on the state of their markets at that same moment.

The character of money as a general form of wealth makes it a suitable means to effect defensive strategies in the face of an uncertain future. It is an asset whose return comes in the form of a liquidity premium rather than a pecuniary compensation. Other assets do not offer the same defence against uncertainty and compensate for this imperfection by paying interest to their holders. Under uncertainty—that is, the possibility that the future will bring unexpected changes—flexibility to adapt to new environments is a gain in itself. That is why people are supposed to prefer to keep their choices open until things become clear enough to allow a proper decision to be made. Liquidity is flexibility. If wealth accumulation is a forward-looking activity, agents will, in principle, prefer to remain liquid. To accept less flexible alternatives, they have to be bribed—that is, they have to be pecuniarily compensated for the reduced liquidity of assets other than money. *The* interest rate, as the representative of this compensation, has to be whatever is necessary to convince agents "to part with liquidity." The higher the degree of illiquidity of an asset, the higher must be, in equilibrium, the compensation paid to convince wealth holders to accept the risks it represents. This mechanism of determination of interest rates is the fundamental statement of liquidity preference theory.

Many Post-Keynesians consider Keynes's discussion of monetary matters in the *Treatise on Money* superior to that presented in *The General Theory*.[4] In the former, Keynes identified two circuits of monetary circulation: industrial circulation and financial circulation.

Industrial circulation refers to the amount of money in use to support the flow of goods and services produced in an economy. The amount of money required to do it depends, naturally, on the average interval during which money is retained between transactions. Keynes distinguished between households and firms for having different habits of payments that implied different velocities of money circulation. Industrial circulation embodies, of course, a view of money very close to that of the quantity theory. Accordingly, Keynes's criticism of the Quantity Theory was not exactly that it was wrong but that it was incomplete because it was not capable of identifying the second circuit of money, the financial circulation. Orthodox theory acknowledged the possibility of hoarding, even though it was on the borderline with irrationality. Keynes's concept of financial circulation went much beyond the notion of hoarding. It dealt with the amount of money used in operations with assets. It included both active balances used to buy and sell assets and inactive balances held in the expectation of future changes in the prices of assets. Confronted with the perspective of future capital losses if interest rates were to rise, wealth holders might prefer to hold money instead. On the other hand, those expecting a fall in future interest rates would buy securities now even if they had to borrow funds to do it. Keynes called the first group bears and the second bulls. Banks would intermediate their operations by accepting deposits from bears and providing loans to bulls to allow them to buy securities. In equilibrium, interest rates would settle at the level in which both bulls and bears would be satisfied with their financial operations.

In *The General Theory*, unfortunately, Keynes downplayed this dichotomy between industrial and financial circulation in favor of a more abstract approach in which an undifferentiated public demands money for various motives. The industrial circulation became the transactions motive and the financial circulation was transformed into the speculative demand for money.[5] The latter was kept as the determinant of interest rates, together with the (exogenously given) money supply.

The analysis of the demand for money for transactions does not involve deep differences between Keynesian analysis and other strands of monetary thought. As was already suggested, on this matter Keynes considered the classics incomplete rather than wrong. On the other hand, the speculative demand was more a development than a radical departure of the ideas contained in the *Treatise*. The concept and its application was made more precise, being utilized to set the price of debts—that is the interest rate, rather than prices of assets in general—allowing Keynes to differentiate, when necessary or adequate, the determination of marginal efficiency of assets from the interest rate (see Kregel, 1988).

The speculative motive is based on the idea of normality that Keynes inherited (and modified) from Marshall. Rejecting the neoclassical notion of a natural rate of interest, rooted in real factors such as time preferences and productivity as an objective gravity center around which market interest rates would move, Keynes suggested instead that every agent operating with assets has a subjective evaluation, given his own experience, of what constitutes a normal rate of interest that is expected to prevail when short-term fluctuations are allowed for. This normal interest rate acts as an anchor to his expectations of future movements of the interest rate and defines whether the agent will be a bear or a bull in face of current interest rates. The latter will be determined at the point in which bulls and bears balance each other, as proposed before in the *Treatise*.

A third motive to hold money, the precautionary motive, is introduced in *The General Theory*, and should also be part of the financial circulation. Keynes gave it, however, a surprisingly superficial treatment since one could argue that it is as a precaution against an uncertain future that money assumes its peculiar role in a monetary economy.[6]

It seems that Keynes was overwhelmed with the difficulty of analyzing the precautionary motive since it required explict consideration of the influence of states of confidence on the demand for money. As Kahn (1972) showed, we can consider the precautionary demand as leading agents to hold buffer stocks of both money and securities in order to avoid both capital and income risks. Wealth holders would recognize that any expectation they may have is liable to fail and would hedge against failing expectations by keeping some reserves of assets that would act as a rear guard for them. In this sense, bulls, for instance, would not commit all their resources to securities unless they expected a future fall of the interest rate with certainty. The combination between speculative and precautionary motives would, thus, mean that the speculative demand has to do with specific expectations as to future movements of the rate of interest and the precautionary motive with the degree of confidence in those expectations.

Finally, in the debates around *The General Theory* following its publication, Keynes introduced a fourth motive to hold money, which he called the finance motive. It was meant to be a bridge between industrial and financial circulation because it refered to balances that are held inactive in advance of the purchase of investment goods. The finance motive should not be considered as part of the transactions demand because of its out-of-routine character that would break the proportionality between income flows and money demand. On the other hand, it was kept with a view to a definite expenditure plan as with other transactions made in the economy. Money was a convenience rather than an asset. Although Keynes made it clear that the finance motive is a reason to demand money, the use of the term finance gave origin to all kinds of equivocations, relating it to savings, to financial relations, and so on, in a debate that was revived very recently.[7]

2. 3. Liquidity Preference as a General Theory of Asset Pricing

The aggregative structure utilized in most of *The General Theory* recognizes two composite assets: money and bonds.[8] In this case we may safely state, as Keynes did that "the rate of interest at any time, being the reward for parting with liquidity, is a measure of the willingness of those who possess money to part with their control over it" (Keynes, 1964, p. 167). Liquidity in *The General Theory* can be associated only with money or with bonds. In this dichotomous world, the interest paid on bonds can only be a compensation for its lower degree of liquidity as compared with money.

Working with only two composite assets had the advantage of making it clear that the true nature of interest resided in its being a compensation for the risk of illiquidity rather than a reward for abstention of consumption per se, which was the classical view of interest. It had, however, two major weaknesses: it made possible for neoclassical-synthesis Keynesians to reduce liquidity preference to simply a formulation of a money demand function, and it could lead less careful readers to ignore that the interest rate was an index related to a composite asset. These less careful interpreters tended to choose arbitrary market rates to serve as the interest rate of *The General Theory*, giving rise to endless but essentially useless (because misdirected) debates as to which rates Keynes had in mind when presenting his money demand theory of his marginal efficiency of capital model of investment.

The neoclassical synthesis was, in general, guilty of both faults, and so were the neoclassical critics of Keynes. Nevertheless, it could be easily seen that liquidity preference could be generalized into a general theory of asset pricing based on the same general principle that different degrees of liquidity should be compensated by pecuniary returns that would define the rate of return obtained for the possession of different assets.[9] As pointed out by Wells (1983, p. 533), liquidity preference is a theory for explaining the spread between the rates of return associated with different assets, an analog to Ricardo's model of differential rents.

One of the first attempts to develop liquidity preference into a theory of asset pricing was by Robinson in 1951(1979). In that work Robinson analyzed in detail the disadvantages that assets other than money would present, classifying them as inconvenience (or "illiquidity in the narrow sense"), capital uncertainty, income uncertainty, and lender's risk ("that is, the fear of partial or total failure of the borrower") (Robinson, 1979, p. 140). Specific assets would be affected by each disadvantage in a different degree, affecting their prices. In her words (1979, p. 143), "These qualities of the various types of asset are differently evaluated by different individuals.... The general pattern of interest rates depends upon the distribution of wealth between owners with different tastes, relatively to the supplies of the various kinds of assets. Each type of asset is a potential alterative to every other; each has, so to speak, a common frontier with every other and with money. Equilibrium in the market is attained when the interest rates are such that no wealth is moving accross any frontier. Prices are then such that the market is content to hold just that quantity of each type of asset which is available at the moment."

That was precisely the solution Keynes had found earlier when dealing with two assets. In fact, a few years after Robinson published her essay, Kahn (1972, p. 73) was able to demonstrate that the speculative demand could be shown to operate when securities of different maturities were considered in precisely the same way Keynes had conceived in *The General Theory*: "If a person is indifferent between bonds and bills, then, apart from considerations of risk, it must mean either that the two rates coincide and he expects the long-term rate to remain constant, or that the rate (measured as a proportional rate per annum) at which he expects the long-term rate of interest to be rising (i.e. the price of bonds to be falling) is equal to the excess of the long-term rate of interest (the rate on bonds, measured as a rate per annum) over the short-term rate of interest (the rate on bills, measured as a rate per annum)—or a similar proportion in terms of an expected fall in the long-term rate of interest if the short-term rate is higher than the long- term rate."

Post-Keynesians have actually extended liquidity preference theory one step further. As Minsky (1975, 1982, 1986) has shown, an agent, when choosing assets to hold, is not restricted by his own original resources. The purchasing power over assets may be complemented by access to credit—that is, when the agent is willing to issue debts. To approach the portfolio strategy of agents, one has then to describe not only his assets but also his liabilities.

In Minsky's model two factors have to be considered if an agent's strategy is to be identified by his whole balance sheet instead of just his assets. One has to determine his solvency, which concerns the question of whether his assets are worth at least as much as his liabilities, and his liquidity position—that is, his capacity to pay his liabilities as they come due with the returns of his assets. In other words, one has to look at the present values of assets and liabilities, but one has also to look at the profiles through which inflows and outflows of cash are expected to take place. Prices of assets depend on the demand for them. The possibility of issuing debts influences the demand for assets. The conditions in which debts can be created will determine the limits to asset demands and, thus, to the return rates offered on each type of asset. Minsky's model of cyclically changing financial fragility is, thus, a generalization of liquidity preference theory to deal also with liabilities.[10]

All these models, beginning with Keynes's Chapter 17 of *The General Theory*, are able to give us short-period solutions for the price of assets, when the quantities of each asset are given, and a long-period solution when the availability of assets is allowed to change. Actually, a Post-Keynesian model of capital accumulation can be derived that can show the conditions under which the production of new capital goods will be stimulated (see Davidson, 1978, ch. 4). In the complete model all privately created assets are allowed to change in order to describe a long-period equilibrium. Nevertheless,

Keynes also postulated that money could not be reproducible as easily as other assets because it would lose its peculiar characteristic of having the greatest liquidity premium of all assets. (Keynes, 1964, p. 241n). In *The General Theory* the quantity of money available is taken as given, insensitive to the demands of the public.

The behavior of the money supply has since become an important bone of contention among Keynesians with some arguing in favor of considering the money supply to be under the control of the monetary authorities and others arguing that the quantity of money should be seen as endogenously determined. Supporters of these two rather extreme positions debate the power of the central bank to oppose market trends, but, with a few exceptions noted later, they seem to forget that most of what exists as money in a modern entrepreneurial economy is actually created by private banks. Nevertheless, surprisingly scanty attention is given to the behavior of banks when the determination of the money supply is examined. Again, one can suggest that banks also act according to their own liquidity preference schedule and that this has important implications for the behavior of the money supply.

2. 4. The Liquidity Preference of Banks

According to Kaldor, Keynes was an exogenist—that is, he believed in the possibility of controlling the quantity of money because he was never able to free himself entirely from classical ideas (Kaldor, 1982). Moore (1988, p. 8) even charges Keynes with discussing a commodity-money economy rather than a modern credit-money economy when he proposed that one fundamental property of money was its low elasticity of production. In the view of these authors, Post-Keynesians should abandon Keynes's treatment of money while keeping his theory of employment.[11]

In this section I will argue in favor of a different view, one that could be seen as a third position between horizontalists and verticalists, defended by authors like Davidson, Kregel, and Dow (Dow, 1987–1988; Dow and Dow, 1989), among others, that is more in agreement not only with Keynes's own writings on the behavior of banks but also with the empirical evidence as to how money markets operate in the real world.

Although Keynes does say in *The General Theory* that the money supply is determined independently of demand, in a modern monetary economy most of what constitutes money is created by private agents. Assets other than the legal tender can become money if there is a market maker strong enough to guarantee its convertibility, at fixed prices, into legal tender. It is precisely because, by custom or by law, the monetary authorities of practically every modern capitalist economy guarantee the convertibility of some specified private liabilities, such as demand deposits at commercial banks, at par to legal tender that these liabilities become money. Thus, the supply of money certainly includes money issued by the authorities and deposits created by banks. If we consider, as Keynes did, that the authorities can control the amount of money they originally create through their investments policy, we must turn to the banks to examine whether money is or is not endogenously created. In Minsky's words, "In our economy, money is created as bankers acquire assets and is destroyed as debtors fulfill their obligations" (Minsky, 1982, p. 17). Or, to quote Chick, "The money supply is mainly the liability of the banking system, not of government. Most monetary policy actions thus rely on the banking system to intermediate between the initial policy action and the final effect on the money supply" (Chick, 1979, pp. 19–20).

Portfolio choices by banks are determined by the need to combine profitability and liquidity. It is from their choices about which assets to buy and liabilities to issue that the supply of money is ultimately determined. In particular, money comes into existence when banks create deposits that are issued to allow assets to be bought by banks from the public, on the occasion, for instance, of providing a loan. In other words, money is created and made available to nonbank agents as a result of the portfolio decisions of banks. The responsiveness of banks to demands from the public depends on the preferences that orient those portfolio decisions.

Banks are intrinsically speculative agents since their assets are typically less liquid than their liabilities. They actually profit from the difference between rates that are paid on their assets and liabilities that reflect the different liquidity premia associated with each component of their balance sheets. It is by exploring probability/liquidity trade-offs that the overall profitability of the banking business is established. The availability of means of payment is decided as a by-product of these choices. Banks can direct their resources to financial circulation (when they buy, for instance, government bonds or bills) or to industrial circulation (if they finance the working capital of firms). Therefore, depending on the choices made by banks, not only can the money supply vary but the relation between the availability of money and aggregate demand can also be different, since, as we have seen, industrial and financial circulations have different connections with the flow of income.

The crucial point is that the most profitable placement for banks is seldom the safest or the most liquid. If uncertainty is high, banks may prefer the liquidity of excess reserves or, more probably, the purchase of government securities rather than run the risks of buying potentially more profitable, but also riskier, private liabilities. The consideration of liquidity preference on the part of banks certainly imparts a feature of endogeneity to the money supply, although one could hardly argue that it makes the supply of money horizontal in the interest and money space. What the approach really suggests is that the very dichotomy between money demand and supply may be too narrow. It is the same fundamental factor that is in operation in both sides of the market: liquidity preference. This led Robinson (1979, p. 21) to state that "the supply of finance cannot be regarded as a rigid bottleneck limiting the rate of investment, but must be treated rather as an element in the general atmosphere encouraging or retarding accumulation."

2.5. Liquidity Preference and Inflationary Environments

Production in monetary economies is organized on the basis of a system of forward contracts that allows entrepreneurs to reduce, at least in part, the uncertainties that plague the future. The role of contracts is to assure the entrepreneur that labor and other inputs necessary for the continuity of the productive activity will be available at the required rates and at prices that justify the decision to produce, oriented by the expectation of profits from the sale of goods in the markets. The existence of a widespread system of contracts serves to anchor the expectations as to the future value of money and to sustain the calculation of prospective advantages that is characteristic of capitalist production.

The importance of contracts in Keynes and Post-Keynesian economics can be hardly exaggerated. As Keynes wrote, "The introduction of a money, in terms of which loans and contracts with a time element can be expressed, is what really changes the economic status of a primitive society" (*CW*, XXVIII, p. 255). The strategic role of contracts gives us the point from which to start when thinking about money: "Now for most important social and economic purposes what matters is the money of account; for it is the money of account which is the subject of contract and of customary obligation" (*CW*, XXVIII, p. 253).

Finally, Keynes could not be more explicit as to the importance of the "convention of stability"—the generalized belief in the stability of the purchasing power of money in the nineteenth century, for the development of the financial relations that allowed capitalism to grow (*CW*, IV).[12]

A Post-Keynesian approach to inflation and, in particular, to persistently high inflation has to start from its effects on the system of contracts, on the definition of the money-of-account and on the implications of these effects on the liquidity preferences of the public.

Inflation erodes the purchasing power of money between two points in time. If a convention of stability survives this erosion, it will be seen as a random occurrence not affecting bona fide contracts. After all, the parties to a contract know that they cannot control all elements influencing the outcome of a given process unfolding over time. Unexpected events—acts of God—can always happen, disappointing one or both parties. Contracts are defences against predictable developments. In a stable-price economy, inflation would be something like a natural accident. It can disappoint expectations in the same sense that other uncontrollable and unpredictable events may. If inflation is not seen as a systematic force operating in the environment, it will probably be ignored by the parties when defining a contract. Society has so much to gain from the existence of a system of forward money contracts that eventual losses, even if heavy at times, do not lead agents to entertain doubts as to the convenience of its maintenance. The money-of-account remains the same, and the liquidity properties of the legal tender and its closest substitutes are preserved.

Persistent creeping inflation changes the situation, but not in an essential way. Systematic but low inflation is a nuisance to contracting parties, obliging them to take special precautions, but it still does not change the relation between the money-of-account and money proper—that is the means of payment. Contracts are still made in terms of money, even if now the parties try to anticipate the erosion that is expected to take place before the settling date. The liquidity properties of money are at least partially retained since the essence of moneyness, as we saw, is conferred by the function of money-of-account that, in these circumstances, is still performed by money.[13]

An essential change takes place when inflation is persistent and high and the potential losses from mistaken expectations as to the future course of prices make it too risky to accept contracts denominated in money. Agents will then search for alternative monies-of-account, which may be either a foreign money, such as the U.S. dollar, or other units of account, indexing contracts to price indices that represent baskets of goods that are meaningful to one or both of the contracting parties. I have examined elsewhere the operation of a monetary economy under hyperinflation or in a high inflation regime (Carvalho, 1991). For the purposes of this essay, what is important to stress is that in these cases money loses practically all its liquidity premium. Now, to hold money is no longer to have the asset in terms of which debts are denominated. Money has to be converted into the unit of contracts, and this exchange rate is as uncertain in advance as any other in the economy. Everybody may expect that the purchasing power of money will fall, but the possibility of wrongly anticipating by how much it will be depreciated involves the risk of heavy losses if one tries to hold money.

Under highly inflationary regimes either financial innovations are created, particularly assets that are denominated in the same unit as contracts are made, or a flight into goods and foreign assets will be unavoidable. Liquidity preference does not disappear with high inflation, but it does change the public's views as to what may constitute an adequate "liquidity time-machine," to use Davidson's expression. A very unstable system may emerge as the public and banks and financial institutions adapt themselves to the existence of multiple units of account.[14]

2.6. Conclusion

In this essay I presented Post-Keynesian developments of the liquidity preference theory. Money is a crucial element of Post-Keynesian economics that is defined precisely by the research around the workings of a monetary economy, defined by Keynes as one in which money is not neutral in the long as in the short period.

Liquidity preference was originally presented as a theory of the interest rate, since it was developed in *The General Theory* in a framework in which only two composite assets, money and bonds, were considered. Posterior developments, mainly due to Robinson and Kahn showed that the scheme was easily generalizable to the determination of the structure of interest rates, by altering the degree of aggregation considered in the model. Minsky advanced one step further by showing that the scheme could be used to explain not only the prices of assets but actually the balance-sheet choices as a whole, including assets and liabilities.

Since most of what exists as money in modern economies is created by banks, we showed that the behavior of the money supply can be approached according to the same principles that explain the behavior of the general public. In opposition to more naive approaches that offer extreme postulates as to the interest elasticity of the money supply curve, we can show that money is at least partially endogenous because it is created as part of the strategies banks use to interact with their environment.

Finally, I dealt with a research subject that is still in its first steps—that is, how persistently high inflation changes the liquidity attributes of assets and of money in particular. Post-Keynesian theory is specially well equipped to study these issues given the role it gives to forward contracts denominated in money in the organization of the economy and the definition of the forms of wealth available for private accumulation.

ACKNOWLEDGEMENTS

I thank my old friend and fellow Post-Keynesian Carmem Aparecida Feijo for the inumerable occasions she discussed with me the subjects presented in this essay. Comments by Paul Wells were most welcome. Financial support from the Brazilian Research Council (CNPq) is gratefully acknowledged. Of course, only I am responsible for any remaining errors.

NOTES

1. The interested reader should look at Volumes 13 and especially 29 of Keynes's *Collected Writings* to follow the author's attempts to give a rigorous analytic form to the concept. A very good and concise presentation of the main features of a monetary economy is found in Kregel (1980).

2. I explored the notion of long period and the role of money in the use Keynes makes of it in Carvalho (1990). On the nonneutrality of money see Davidson (1978) and Davidson and Kregel (1980).

3. But Keynes did not neglect the analysis of bank choices in the *Treatise*. Quite the opposite, Keynes developed a scheme for approaching banks' choices about how to balance profitability and liquidity in their portfolios (See *CW*, VI, ch. 25). I will return to this theme in Section 2.4.

4. For a dissenting voice, see Minsky (1975).

5. For a detailed examination of the transition between the bears and bulls of the *Treatise* to the demand for money and the demand for other assets in *The General Theory*, see Kregel (1988). For a discussion of the origins of the notion of liquidity prefence as a model for asset choice, see Kregel (1984).

6. According to Keynes the precautionary motive is "to provide for contingencies requiring sudden expenditure and for unforeseen opportunities of advantageous purchase, and also to hold an asset of which the value is fixed in terms of money" (Keynes, 1964, p. 196). The latter element means to be able to settle debts when necessary.

7. See Asimakopulos (1983), Kregel (1984–1985), Asimakopulos (1986), Kregel (1986), and Davidson (1986), which were, among other essays, the main contributions to this discussion. For a very good and clear account of the finance motive, see Chick (1983, pp. 198–200). See also Wells (1981).

8. Sometimes bonds and capital goods are fused together, as in parts of Chapter 12. In the *Treatise* this confusion was widespread and gave origin to criticisms even from Keynes's most intimate colaborators. See, for instance, Kahn's letters to Keynes (*CW*, XIII). One should notice, on the other hand, that money is a composite asset too. See Keynes (1964 p. 167, n. 1).

9. As a matter of fact, Keynes himself did it in *The General Theory*, in Chapter 17, where he dealt with many assets instead of only two and built a model of asset pricing based on the attributes of assets, including liquidity premia accruing to diverse assets in different degrees, in his own rates-of-interest scheme.

10. Minsky (1975) actually uses Keynes's rates-of-interest model and notation to present his own version of the balance-sheet choices that accompany wealth accumulation.

11. These authors do not make it clear to what extent this should mean the abandonment of the whole liquidity preference theory or the notions of uncertainty, the role of expectations, and so on.

12. Weintraub echoes most of these concerns in his writings. See, for instance, Weintraub (1978).

13. Actually, money tends to lose some of its liquidity premium because financial institutions and banks try to introduce financial innovations that will attract wealth holders to strengthen their competitive position. Since the bait offered by these new financial instruments is some hedge against inflation, interest rates tend to rise, although not necessarily as much as inflation itself. Keynes's criticisms of the Fisher theory of nominal interest rates as well as Davidson's discussion of the most recent versions of that theory assume a situation where no such policies are implemented and no choices are offered to wealth holders (see Keynes, 1964, p. 142; Davidson, 1981).

14. A very interesting and well-informed illustration of these effects for the case of Brazil is found in Feijo (1991).

REFERENCES

Asimakopulos, Athanasios. (1983). "Kalecki and Keynes on Finance, Investment and Saving." *Cambridge Journal of Economics*, 7(3–4), 22–233.

———. (1986). "Finance, Liquidity, Saving and Investment." *Journal of Post Keynesian Economics*, 9(1), 70–90.

Carvalho, F. (1990). "Keynes and the Long Period." *Cambridge Journal of Economics*, 14(3).

———. (1991) "A Post Keynesian Approach to Inflation, High Inflation and Hyperinflation." In P. Davidson and J. Kregel (Eds.), *Economic Problems of the 1990's*. Aldershot, U. K.: Elgar.

Chick, Victoria. (1979). *The Theory of Monetary Policy*. Oxford: Basil Blackwell.

———. (1983). *Macroeconomics after Keynes*. Cambridge, MA: The MIT Press.

Davidson, Paul. (1978). *Money and the Real World* (2nd Ed.). London: Macmillan.

———. (1981). "A Critical Analysis of Monetarist–Rational Expectation–Supply-Side (Incentive) Economics Approach to Accumulation during a Period of Inflationary Expectations." *Kredit und Kapital*, 14(4), 496–504.

———. (1986). "Finance, Funding, Saving and Investment." *Journal of Post Keynesian Economics*, 9(1), 101–110.

Davidson, Paul and J. Kregel. (1980). "Keynes's Paradigm: A Theoretical Framework for Monetary Analysis." In E. Nell (Ed.), *Growth, Profits and Property*. New York: Cambridge University Press.

Dow, Sheila. (1987–1988). "Post Keynesian Monetary Theory for an Open Economy." *Journal of Post Keynesian Economics*, 9(2), 237–257.

Dow, A. and S. Dow. (1989). "Endogenous Money Creation and Idle Balances." In J. Pheby (Ed.), *New Directions in Post-Keynesian Economics*. Aldershot, U. K.: Elgar.

Feijo, Carmem. (1991). "Economic Growth and Inflation in Brazil in the 1970s: A Post Keynesian Interpretation," Ph.D. dissertation, University of London.

Kahn, Richard. (1972). "Some Notes on Liquidity Preference." In R. Kahn (Ed.), *Selected Essays on Employment and Growth*, Cambridge: Cambridge University Press. Originally published in 1954.

Kaldor, Nicholas, (1982). *The Scourge of Monetarism*. Oxford: Oxford University Press.

Keynes, John Maynard. (1964). *The General Theory of Employment, Interest and Money*. New York: Harcourt, Brace, Jovanovich.

———. *The Collected Writings of John Maynard Keynes*. London: Macmillan and Cambridge: Cambridge University Press. Volumes are referred to by CW followed by the volume number in Roman numerals.

Kregel, Jan. (1980). "Markets and Institutions as Features of a Capitalistic Production System." *Journal of Post Keynesian Economics*, 3(1), 3–48.

———. (1984). "Expectations and Rationality within a Capitalist Framework." In E. Nell (Ed.), *Free Market Conservatism*. London: George Allen and Unwin.

———. (1984–1985). "Constraints on the Expansion of Output and Employment: Real or Monetary." *Journal of Post Keynesian Economics*, 7(2),13–52.

———. (1986). "A Note on Finance, Liquidity, Saving and Investment." *Journal of Post Keynesian Economics*, 9(1), 91–100.

———. (1988). "Irving Fisher, Great-Grandparent of the General Theory: Money, Rate of Return over Cost and Efficiency of Capital." *Cahiers d'Economie Politique*, 14(5).

Minsky, Hyman. (1975). *John Maynard Keynes*. New York: Columbia University Press.

———. (1982). *Can 'It' Happen Again?* Armonk, N. Y.: M.E. Sharpe.

———. (1986). *Stabilizing an Unstable Economy*. New Haven, CT: Yale University Press.

Moore, Basil, (1988). *Horizontalists and Verticalists: The Macroeconomics of Credit Money*, Cambridge: Cambridge University Press.

Robinson, Joan, (1979). "The Rate of Interest." In J. Robinson (Ed.), *The Generalization of the General Theory and Other Essays*. London: Macmillan. First published in 1951.

Shackle, George L.S. (1968). "Recent Theories Concerning the Nature and Role of Interest." In *Surveys of Economic Theory*, London: Macmillan. First published in 1961.

Weintraub, Sidney. (1978). *Capitalism's Inflation and Unemployment Crisis*, Reading, MA: Addison Wesley.

Wells, Paul. (1981). "Keynes' Demand for Finance." *Journal of Post Keynesian Economics*, 3(4), 586–589.

———. (1983). "A Post Keynesian View of Liquidity Preference and the Demand for Money." *Journal of Post Keynesian Economics*, 5(4), 52–536.

3

FIRM-DETERMINED PRICES: THE POST-KEYNESIAN CONCEPTION

NINA SHAPIRO AND TRACY MOTT

While Keynes accepted the price theory of the classical school, his market system was not the impersonal, deterministic one of classical and neoclassical economics.[1] Entrepreneurial expectations mattered; the operations of the enterprise were not decided by the market. It was the expected output price, not the currently obtainable one, that determined the employment offered in the enterprise, and while the prices of the day did affect the short-run expectations of entrepreneurs, they did not determine the long-run expectations. These changed not with the state of the market but with the confidence in its outcomes, and long-run expectations decided the equilibrium employment and output.

The importance of enterprise decisions distinguishes Keynesian theory, and in its Kaleckian formulation, these decisions affect the prices of products as well as their rates of production. Here, it is not the auctioneer but the product's producer that decides the product price. The firm has the market power needed to mark up the price of its product and raise it above the product's costs. The price decisions of the firm are effective, and it is because the price decided on by the enterprise is the one realized in the market that the price theory of the Kaleckian tradition centers on the product pricing of the enterprise.

This Post-Keynesian theory is examined in this chapter, with the view of determining the distinctiveness of the mark-up price conception. Kalecki's own formulation of the conception is considered, along with its development in the works of Steindl, Eichner, and others. Of special concern is the treatment of the firm, which is shown to be quite different from the traditional one, and the root of the differences between Post-Keynesian and classical price theory.

3.1. Prices and Costs

The mark-up price of the Post-Keynesian theory is a cost-based value. It is rooted in the expenses of the product's production, which place a floor under its level. But while the price depends on the product's costs, it is not determined by them. It varies with the mark-up on the costs, and this profit margin is not given by the requisites of the product's production or the technology that underlies its costs.

The mark-up that connects the product price to the product costs is a decision variable. It is determined by the product's producer and depends on the objectives of the firm's product pricing. These ends decide the relation between the product price and costs; they determine the extent to which changes in the costs are incorporated in the price, along with the flexibility of its level. Changes in the price depend on their effects on the enterprise, and while the price can shift with the product's costs, it will do so if and only if the price change serves the ends of the enterprise.

The mark-up price is firm determined rather than cost (or demand) determined, and it is the firm's determination of the price that relates it to the product's costs. It depends on the costs not because the product must be reproduced, but because the firm's expenditure on it must be recouped. The revenue for the firm's operations comes from the sale of its products, and if the prices of these are "too low in relation to their costs," then the revenue will fall short of the firm's requirements (Kalecki, 1971, ch. 5).

For the product revenue to be high enough for the operation of the enterprise, the product price must cover the product costs, and this requires the pricing of the product on the basis of its costs. The mark-up price is formed out of the product's costs, through a mark-up on them, because it is formed by the firm, with its ends in mind. And, indeed, if the price were not decided by the enterprise—if it were determined, instead, in the market for the product—the price would have no determinate relation to the costs of the product's production.

When the product is priced in the market, its price depends on the particularities of its sale rather than those of its production. The product supply and demand, at the time and place of the product's exchange, decide the price. Its level is bid up and down until the product offers and bids are equilibrated, and the price that sells out the product supply can be greater or less than the cost of the product's production.

The market-clearing price is not a cost-clearing one, and while it may equal the product's costs in the long run, it will cover them only by accident in the short one. The natural (cost) levels of the market's prices are realized when, and only when, the long-period equilibrium is achieved; and when the prices are not in their equilibrium relationship, the price of any product can be less than the expenses of its production. All firms can suffer losses, and even the efficient ones can go under.

The problem, here, is not just that the market-clearing price may not be high enough for the funding of the firm's operations. It is also that the firm has no way of knowing whether, or when, the price will be high enough. The market for the product may or may not clear at a price that covers the product's costs, and the fact that it clears at a price that is favorable to the firm at one point of time does not mean that it will do so at another, or even at the next.

The market's prices are erratic as well as flexible, and, indeed, they are erratic because they are flexible. Their responsiveness to supply-and-demand shifts makes their levels fickle and uncertain, and when product prices are unpredictable, the luck of the draw decides which of the enterprises survive. The firms that succeed are the ones that happen to be operating in excess demand markets, and the enterprises that make it through one market period may be forced out of operation by the changes that occur in another.

The firm's existence is precarious when it is subject to the market's prices (Levine, 1980); and while the firm might be able to withstand the vagaries of these prices if its resources were malleable, neither the physical nor the human ones are. The equipment is product-specific as well as site-specific; it cannot be wheeled in and out of different lines of production (Williamson, 1985) or sold without loss when the revenue from its use falls off. And while the labor that operates the machinery may be dispensable, the labor that plans and directs its utilization is not. The enterprise cannot operate without a management—it is not a production function—and the knowledge and skills of its managers, as well as those of its engineers and product designers, cannot be changed overnight.

The restructuring of the enterprise takes both time and money, and when its existing operations fail, the funds needed for the development of new ones will not be there. The firm will not be able to move into a more profitable line of production or supply the kinds of products that the market requires. The result of the market's disciplines will not be the improvement of the enterprise but its demise.

Survival in the market requires market power; the enterprises that survive the market are the ones that can affect its outcomes. They are the firms with the size and financial strength needed to wait out the market and stabilize its results, the ones that can hold up the prices of their products through output (or inventory) adjustments and maintain their sales through the differentiation of their products. These monopolistic enterprises are the kind that can live to the long run, and they can operate in the long period precisely because their revenues are secure in the short period.

The market power of the enterprise is the central concern of the Post-Keynesian theory, which takes in its importance and draws out its price implications. The prices derived in the mark-up models of the theory are not the prices that serve the unconscious ends of the market (the allocative efficiency of the neoclassical theory or the systemic reproduction of the Ricardian conception), but the ones that serve the conscious ends of the enterprise. They are administered values, and it is because the prices are firm determined that they cover the costs of production.

3.2. The Degree of Monopoly

When the product price is firm determined, it depends first on the market objectives of the enterprise—the ends that it pursues in its product pricing—and second on the market environment in which the firm operates. While the product need not be sold at the price that clears the market, the revenue from its sale does depend on the market's properties. It depends on the product demand and the competition for that demand; and because these condition the product's sale, they affect the price and constrain the pricing power of the enterprise.

The market constraints on the firm are highlighted in Kalecki's theory, where the pricing power of the enterprise is a matter of degree. It is limited by the competition in the market for the product, and while the firm can mark up the product's price, the mark-up on the product's costs cannot be too high. The firm has to consider the sales effects of the mark-up's level, for higher mark-ups mean higher prices; and when the firm's price is above that of its competitors, sales are lost, and the revenue from the product can drop.

The sales effects of the mark-up depend on the competitive strength of the enterprise. When its monopoly power is great, when it has secured a large share of the industry output, the sales loss that accompanies a price increase will be small. The degree of the firm's monopoly determines the price elasticity of the demand for its product, and under the constant cost conditions of Kalecki's theory, this price elasticity marks out the profit that can be realized at different levels of the product price.

The price that maximizes the profit is given by the degree of monopoly, while the excess of this price over the product's costs measures the monopoly. Because the competitive profit-maximizing price equals the product's costs (the marginal ones), the monopoly power of the firm is reflected in the difference between these costs and the profit-maximizing price. This difference is the profit margin that is given with the degree of monopoly, and as the level of this monopoly margin increases, so does the profit that can be made on the product.

The degree of monopoly determines the maximum level of the profit; the profit on the product cannot be greater than the amount entailed in the monopoly margin. But while the profit cannot be greater than the monopoly amount, it can be less. The mark-up on the product need not be as high as the degree of monopoly, and while it is in the case of Kalecki's theory, this is not because Kalecki's firm has to profit maximize.

While the competitive firm must maximize its profits—it cannot survive, otherwise—the monopolistic one does not need to make the highest possible amount. It can afford a lower than maximum profit, for its assets and goodwill secure its revenues and extend its credit. If it makes less on a sale than the market allows, it will not go under; and the revenue that can be made on the sales of the day is not the only profit that it can count on. The profit foregone today can be made up tomorrow, and because the amount made on any particular sale is not essential to the enterprise—it can survive whatever the level of the profit, and even if it is a negative amount—the monopolistic firm does not have to charge the profit-maximizing price.

The monopolistic firm has a choice of prices; it is a price-maker, not a price-taker. It decides the price, and, indeed, it is its ability to do so that distinguishes its operations from those of the competitive firm. The monopoly power of the firm is reflected in its price choice, and the greater its price choices, the higher its degree of monopoly.

3.3. Profit Maximization

The profit-maximizing price is not necessarily optimal. The desirability of any particular level of the price depends on the ends that the price serves, and in the case of the monopolistic firm, price levels other than the profit-maximizing one are not only feasible and profitable, they are also more desirable.

Profit maximization is rational when, and only when, the objective of the enterprise is the exploitation of its market. This is the end that is realized with the profit-maximizing price, for the profit that is maximized in the price is the profit of the here and now. It is the profit that can be made under the existing conditions in the industry and on the basis of the position that the firm has already achieved within it.

But the profit of the day is not the only profit that counts. The profit of tomorrow also matters, and the price that maximizes the profits of today affects the ones of tomorrow. The firm has to consider the long-run effects of its pricing decisions, and it is because Kalecki's firm does not do so that it charges the profit-maximizing price (or what is expected to be the profit-maximizing one).

Kalecki's firm does not worry about the future; it takes its position in the industry for granted and prices its products without any regard for the market-share consequences of its decisions. The prices entertained by the enterprise include ones that shift sales to competitors: as long as the price is profitable—does not drastically reduce sales—its level is acceptable. Sales are traded for profits, with the firm risking its market for the sake of the profit, and just as the protection of its market is not a pricing objective, neither is the expansion.

Kalecki's firm rests on its competitive laurels. It accepts its position in the industry, just as its competitors accept theirs. The competitive conditions in the industry are taken as given, and while the firms exploit their competitive positions, getting as much profit as they can from them, they do not try to strengthen them. The firms make the most of their situations instead of trying to change or improve them: they profit maximize.

Profit-maximizing behavior is adaptive, and the firms that adjust and adapt are not the firms that mark up their prices. They are the firms that have to take whatever price the market will bear—the ones that have no market power. These competitive firms are the ones that take the conditions of the market as given and make the best of their positions within it; and while profit maximization is both natural and rational in the case of the firm that cannot affect the market, it is neither in the case of the firm that can.

The monopolistic firm can price for the future; its pricing power can be executed in the interests of its long-term survival. Market protection and expansion can be the ends of its product pricing, and if they are not, the firm will not have its pricing power for long. If the firm's price does not protect its market—if it induces entry or brings other firms into the market—or undermines goodwill, the monopoly power of the firm will be lost.[2]

While the firm cannot ignore the constraints of its market, it need not accept them either. Its product pricing can be strategic rather than adaptive, and when it is, the market constraints are not determining. The mark-up is not given with the degree of monopoly, for while the degree of monopoly limits the profit on the product, it does not, in this case, determine the amount sought. The firm does not profit maximize, and its ends rather than the market's decide the mark-up on the product.[3]

3.4. Growth and Survival

While the mark-up is decided in the short run, the firm that decides its level looks to the long run. The product pricing of the firm is forward looking and strategic, and because it is, the results of the pricing cannot be determined under the confines of the short run. The setting of the analysis has to be the long run one of market growth and structural development.[4]

This long-run analysis is developed in the works of Steindl (1952, 1990) and Eichner (1976, 1991). These take the price theory of Kalecki into the long run, changing its conditions and overcoming its limitations. The profit-maximization assumption is dropped, and both the cost base of the mark-up price and the ends that the price serves are brought into line with the long-run perspective of the enterprise. The costs that are marked up become the full costs of the product—the long-run unit costs rather than the short-run prime ones—while the pricing ends of the firm become the long-run ones of investment and market expansion. Growth maximization replaces the profit maximization of Kalecki's firm, and the requisites of firm growth determine the mark-up on the product.

While the profit of the firm is not maximized in its price, the amount realized is a critical concern of both Steindl's firm and Eichner's. The growth of the enterprise depends on the profit, for the growth has to be financed, and access to external finance is limited. Assets are needed for the borrowings of the firm, and its equity will be worthless if its operations are not profitable. And because the capital of the firm limits its borrowings and the external financing of its expansion is riskier than the internal financing, the profit of the enterprise provides the bulk of its investment funds.[5]

While profit is needed for the expansion of the enterprise, growth is needed for the survival. The market share of the firm has to be protected—its market power and security rest on it—and market protection requires investment. The output capacity of the firm has to expand in step with the market, the plant and equipment have to be modernized, and the product developed and improved. The firm cannot survive to the long run without investing in its product and production process, and because the life-time of its product is finite—industries decline and products die—investment in new lines of production is also required.[6]

If the firm does not grow, it will not make the profit of tomorrow. Firm growth is the long-run expression of the profit drive of the enterprise; and while the firm cannot maximize its long-run profit (there is no such profit), it can try to increase its profits. It can maximize the rate at which its profits grow over time.[7]

This profit growth is the pricing objective of Eichner's firm. The growth rate that is maximized in its product price is the growth rate of its net revenue (cash flow). This net revenue is increased through investment, with the extent of the increase dependent on the profitability of the investment, and the financial requisites of the investment tie the determination of its level to that of the mark-up on the product.

Increases in the mark-up increase the funds available for investment, and while an increase in the mark-up has its costs, these are not incurred in the short run, at the same time as the increase is effected. The costs of a mark-up increase are those of increased competition in the industry, or the entry effect of the increase, product substitution or the rise in the product price reduces the cost competitiveness of the product, and government intervention in the affairs of the enterprise or industry. None of the negative effects of the mark-up increase will necessarily occur: the costs of the increase are all probable, and all of the effects take time to develop.

Industry entry requires investment, as does product substitution on the part of producers. Consumption preferences are habitual, and changes in government regulations are time-consuming as well as costly. The entry, product substitution, and political effects of a mark-up increase are long-run ones, and until they occur, the increase raises the profit on the product, and the firm has the use of the funds that the increase generates.

Because the costs of a mark-up increase are incurred after the benefits are obtained, the costs are interest costs. They are the implicit interest on the funds that the increase generates and are treated as such in the determination of the mark-up on the product.

In deciding the increase in the mark-up, the firm weighs the interest on the funds from a mark-up increase against the profit that can be made with them. The profit depends on the investment opportunities of the enterprise (the marginal efficiency of investment), while the interest depends on the political environment and degree of monopoly. The pricing power of the firm determines the entry and substitution effects of any given increase in the mark-up, and the increase that is chosen by the enterprise is the one that maximizes the growth of its profit.[8]

Eichner's firm uses its pricing power strategically. The mark-up is raised when funds are needed for growth and survival, and it is because the firm does not exploit its monopoly power—charge the profit-maximizing price—that the mark-up can be raised when the growth of the firm requires it. The product pricing of the firm is a part of its growth strategy, and the investment and mark-up of the firm are determined together, in the same decision process.[9]

3.5. Market Development

While the financial requisites of firm growth are the determining ones in Eichner's price theory, the market requisites are decisive in the case of Steindl's. Here, the product pricing of the firm is aggressive; it serves the ends of market share expansion. When the output growth that the firm can finance is greater than the growth of its market, the firm invades the markets of its competitors. It grows at their expense, with the product pricing of the firm aimed at the capture of their markets and bankruptcy of their operations.

The differences in the pricing behavior of Steindl's and Eichner's firms reflect the differences in their market environments. While Eichner's firm is as growth oriented as Steindl's, it operates under very different conditions, and the conditions under which the product is priced also matter. They affect the pricing ends of the firm, as well as the way in which these are carried out (the price levels that realize the ends).

In the case of Eichner's firm, the conditions of the product pricing are those of an oligopolistic industry. The firms in Eichner's industry are both few in number and large in size. Their production costs are similar, as is their staying power. None of the firms can out price any of the others; and when the cost differentials in an industry are insignificant and all of its members are large enough to withstand price wars, price competition is ineffective. Price leadership develops, competition shifts from the price of the product to its properties and technology, and while the firms in the industry can still grow at the expense of each other, they cannot do so through their product pricing. Price cuts cannot enlarge the market share of Eichner's firm.

The situation is quite different in the case of Steindl's firm, and, indeed, it is the exact opposite. Steindl's firm operates in an imperfectly competitive industry rather than a concentrated one. There are many firms in the industry, and significant differences in the production costs, market shares, and financial security of its members. The largest firms have the lowest costs (highest profit margins) and greatest staying power, while the smallest firms are small enough to be marginal. Their markets can be won in a price war, and when the largest firms want to grow faster than the industry, they can price the smallest firms out.

The product pricing of the progressive (large) firms enlarge their market share, and because their pricing bankrupts the smallest firms, it concentrates the industry. Industry concentration is the other side of price competition, and the degree of monopoly is an outgrowth of the pricing process. It is affected by the mark-up on the product, increasing with the mark-up reductions that concentrate the industry, and because the degree of monopoly is changed through the product pricing of the enterprise, it is determined in the same process as the mark-up on the product.[10]

The aggressive pricing of Steindl's firm develops both its market and its market power, and the conditions under which the product pricing of the firm can expand its market are more general than the ones considered in Steindl (1952). As is shown in Levine (1981, 1988), the firms that operate in new and developing industries have the same price options as the firms that operate in competitive ones. Their markets can be expanded through aggressive pricing, for the demand for new and developing goods is price elastic.

Unlike the market for the mature product, the market for the new one has not yet been saturated. New customers can be brought into the market, and product price reductions can effect their entrance. Price cuts can draw in both new income groups and the purchasers of substitute products. New products compete with old ones, and they also compete with each other, for the uncommitted income of consumers; and because their affordability and cost competitiveness is critical to their development, the requisites of market growth determine the mark-up on the products.[11]

When the firm operates in a new or competitive industry, its product pricing affects both the product demand and competition for that demand (the degree of monopoly). The market conditions that limit the mark-up change with its level, and while the pricing power of the firm is still limited, the market constraints are not binding. They are overcome through the investment and product pricing of the enterprise.

3.6. Strategic Prices

While the prices of the market are equilibrating, the prices of the firm are not. These prices change, rather than reconcile, the conditions under which they are formed. They affect the product supply and demand, and because they are directed at them—determined strategically—they cannot be treated with the static, equilibrium methods of the classics.

The mark-up prices of the Post-Keynesian theory are disequilibrating. They expand markets, concentrate industries, and develop new ones. This structural change is inherent in the mark-up pricing of products, and it is the structural transformation that comes with this pricing that gives it its significance and the Post-Keynesian theory its distinctiveness.

3.7. Macroeconomic Effects

Currently there is a widespread notion that Keynes's argument for unemployment depends on imperfect competition. This is a corollary of the view that Keynesian macroeconomics relies on sticky money wages or prices to achieve underemployment equilibrium. Keynes (1964) however, was clear to assume perfect competition, wherein marginal cost equals price, and to show that his results would be overcome by only money wage or price flexibility in special cases.

While the macro effects of imperfect competition are significant, they have little, if anything, to do with the inflexibility of product price levels. Firm-determined prices are not rigid; they change with the conditions of the product pricing process. And when these impede the aggressive (competitive) pricing of products, it is not the rigidity of the prices that hampers economic recoveries, but the rigidity of the price-cost margins. The aggregate demand effects of product price changes depend on the real wage effects, for it is the distribution of the community's income between profits and wages that determines the saving propensity and so governs consumption expenditure in both the short and long runs (Kalecki, 1971; Kaldor, 1956).

Falling money wages matched by falling prices will do nothing to raise aggregate demand. With no increase in the real wage, consumption out of wages will not expand, and while the deflation will increase the real value of money balances, it will also raise the real value of money debts. Deflation enriches creditors (rentiers) at the expense of debtors (producers and consumers), and under the conditions of a rising enterprise (and consumer) debt burden and increasing bankruptcy rate, the real balance effect will not be operative (Kalecki, 1944; and Keynes, 1964, ch. 19).

The effective demand is not price elastic, and when investment falls below its full employment level, consumption can redress the shortfall in demand only if income is shifted from profits to wages. This, however, will not occur unless price mark-ups decline, and it is their elasticity rather than that of money wages or prices that matters in the macrodynamics of the economy (Kalecki, 1969, ch. 5).[12]

Instead of explaining the involuntary unemployment of the system, the imperfection of its markets explains the dynamism. The product pricing of the firm affects both the level and structure of the aggregate demand, and when the pricing behavior of the firm is strategic rather than adaptive, the macroeconomic conditions change with the price decisions. Neither the saving propensity nor the marginal efficiency of investment can be taken as given, and the macroanalysis has to be as long run and dynamic as the microeconomic one.

ACKNOWLEDGEMENTS

We would like to acknowledge helpful discussions with Malcolm Sawyer, while absolving him of any responsibility for our final product.

NOTES

1. This owes something to Marshall, whose version of neoclassicism, with its use of partial equilibrium and period analysis and its attention to the fixed nature of capital, led his students towards an approach to pricing decisions much different than that tending to come out of Walras (cf. Davidson, 1978, ch. 3).

2. For the importance of entry-prevention, and its product pricing requisites, see Bain (1971) and Sylos-Labini (1969).

3. For an extended discussion of profit maximization, and its relation to the perfect competition of the neoclassical tradition, see Galbraith (1967).

4. This is emphasized in Steindl's discussion of the limitations of Kalecki's price analysis (Steindl, 1987). Also see Levine (1985), which brings out the importance of the time frame of the enterprise and the distinctiveness of the long-run view.

5. This idea was originally formulated by Kalecki (1937) as the principle of increasing risk. See also Mott (1985–1986).

6. The importance of investment in enterprise survival is emphasized in Eichner (1976).

7. Since the long-run is not a particular period of time, the profit that can be made in it is not a determinable amount. The profit of the day is the only kind that can be maximized.

8. While the mark-up will increase with the net investment of the enterprise, it will not decrease when the investment falls off. The price effects of the investment changes are not symmetrical,

for Eichner's firm is an oligopolist, and an oligopolist cannot cut its price without the risk of a ruinous price war.

9. This simultaneous determination of investment and the mark-up is also found in the mark-up price model of Harcourt and Kenyon (1976) and in the profit theory of Wood (1975).

10. For a more detailed discussion of Steindl's theory, see Shapiro (1981).

11. For a discussion of the relation between Levine's price theory and Steindl's see Shapiro (1981), and for a mark-up model that integrates their results, as well as those of Eichner's, see the industry development model of Ong (1981).

12. Mark-ups are downwardly elastic under the cost conditions of Steindl's competitive industry, and when these are not in place, recessions will depress investment instead of profit margins. For an extended discussion see Steindl (1952, chs. 9 and 10).

REFERENCES

Bain, Joe. (1971). *Barriers to New Competition*. Cambridge, MA: Harvard University Press.

Davidson, Paul. (1978). *Money and the Real World* (2nd ed.). New York: Wiley.

Eichner, Alfred. (1976). *The Megacorp and Oligopoly*. Cambridge: Cambridge University Press.

———. (1991). *The Macrodynamics of Advanced Market Economies*. Armonk, NY: Sharpe.

Galbraith, John Kenneth. (1967). *The New Industrial State*. Boston: Houghton Mifflin.

Harcourt, G. C., and P. Kenyon. (1976). "Pricing and the Investment Decision." *Kyklos*, 29, 449–477.

Kaldor, Nicholas. (1956). "Alternative Theories of Distribution." *Review of Economic Studies*, 23, 83–101.

Kalecki, Michal. (1937). "The Principle of Increasing Risk." *Economica*, 4, 440–447.

———. (1944). "Professor Pigou on 'The Classical Stationary State: A Comment." *Economic Journal*, 54, 131–132.

———. (1969). *Studies in the Theory of Business Cycles*. New York: Kelley.

———. (1971). *Selected Essays on the Dynamics of the Capitalist Economy*. Cambridge: Cambridge University Press.

Keynes, John Maynard. (1964). *The General Theory of Employment, Interest, and Money*. New York: Harcourt Brace Johanovich. Originally published in 1936.

Levine, David. (1980). "Aspects of the Classical Theory of the Market." *Australian Economic Papers*, 19, 1–15.

———. (1981). *Economic Theory* (Vol. 2). London: Routledge and Kegan Paul.

———. (1985). "On the Analysis of Advanced Capitalist Economy." In S. Resnick and R. Wolff, (Eds). *Rethinking Marxism: Essays for Harry Magdoff and Paul Sweezy*. Brooklyn, NY: Autonomedia, 205–222.

———. (1988). *Needs, Rights, and the Market*. Boulder, CO: Rienner.

Mott, Tracy. (1985–1986). "Kalecki's Principle of Increasing Risk and the Relation among Mark-up Pricing, Investment Fluctuations, and Liquidity Preference." *Economic Forum*, 15, 65–76.

Ong, Nai-Pew. (1981). "Target Pricing, Competition, and Growth." *Journal of Post Keynesian Economics*, 4, 101–116.

Shapiro, Nina. (1981). "Pricing and the Growth of the Firm." *Journal of Post Keynesian Economics*,

4, 85–100.

Steindl, Josef. (1952). *Maturity and Stagnation in American Capitalism*. Oxford: Basil Blackwell.

———. (1987). "Kalecki's Theory of Pricing: Notes on the Margin." In G. Fink, G. Polli, and M. Riese, (Eds). *Economic Theory, Political Power and Social Justice*. New York: Springer Verlag. Reprinted in Josef Steindl. (1990). *Economic Papers, 1941–88*. New York: St. Martin's Press.

———. (1990). *Economic Papers, 1941–88*. New York: St. Martin's Press.

Sylos-Labini, Paolo. (1969). *Oligopoly and Technical Progress*. Cambridge, MA: Harvard University Press.

Williamson, Oliver E. (1985). *Economic Institutions of Capitalism: Firms, Markets, Relational Contracting*. New York: Free Press.

Wood, Adrian. (1975). *A Theory of Profits*. Cambridge: Cambridge University Press.

4

THE MONETARY AND THE REAL: SECTORAL INTERDEPENDENCE AND MARKET OUTCOMES

DOUGLAS VICKERS

> *"There are good reasons to think that the nature of money is not yet rightly understood."*
>
> John Law, 1720

4.1.

Among the "unsettled questions of political economy," to adapt the title of John Stuart Mill's important but neglected *Essays*,[1] none is more pressing at the present time, or more important for aggregate analysis and policy, than that of the relation between the monetary and the real. The "veil of money," the notion that money was neutral, and the "axiom of reals" or the preoccupation with real activity that took place behind the monetary veil, have heavily influenced the development of economic analysis. Not only is that true in a historic sense; it continues to haunt modern constructions (see Silk, 1984). The observation of John Law that heads this chapter had immediate reference, of course, to the progress in the theory of money that occurred in the eighteenth century (see Vickers, 1959; Hutchinson, 1988). But the questions implicit in the statement have continuing relevance for contemporary opinion and the functioning of the monetary economy.

My objective in this chapter is to consider the relation between the availability of money, the circulation of it, and the determination of real values and rates of progress in real incomes in the economy. Following the inspiration of Keynes, recent literature has examined the relation between finance, investment, and saving and has considered the extent to which connections exist between the real expansion implicit in potential multiplier effects on the one hand and the familiar notion of the velocity of circulation of money on the other.[2] Tsiang (1956, p. 563), in an early article, concluded that "in considering the effects of inflationary financing of development investment, the multiplier principle, *which neglects the supply of money and the money-market mechanism*, can be dangerously misleading." More recently Snippe (1985, p. 267), basing his argument on the increase in the demand for money and finance that results from the multiplier process, has observed that it "does not alleviate the finance problem, but, rather makes it worse."

My immediate perspective is influenced by Keynes's post-*General Theory* argument that

> if [following an increase in investment expenditure] there is no change in the liquidity position, the public can save ex-ante and ex-post and ex-anything else until they are blue in the face, without alleviating the problem in the least—unless, indeed, the result of their efforts is to lower the scale of activity to what it was before . . . .*The banks hold the key position in the transition from a lower to a higher scale of activity*. If they refuse to relax, the growing congestion of the short-term loan market or the new issue market, as the case may be, will inhibit the improvement, no matter how thrifty the public purpose to be out of their future income . . . .*The investment market can become congested through shortage of cash*. It can never become congested through shortage of savings. This is the most fundamental of my conclusions within this field. (Keynes, 1937a, pp. 668–669, italics added.)

In *The General Theory* (though I am not setting out to present an exegesis of that work), Keynes had argued similarly that "if the grant of a bank credit to an entrepreneur additional to the credits already existing allows him to make an addition to current investment which would not have otherwise occurred, incomes will necessarily be increased and at a rate which will normally exceed the rate of increased investment. Moreover, except in conditions of full employment, there will be an increase of real income as well as of money-income." This is, of course, the familiar real multiplier process. But Keynes has here supposed that its instigation depends on an initial "grant of bank credit" or the creation of new money. It follows, in ways we shall examine more fully, that saving in a unique monetary sense will increase as a result of the new money creation. "The savings which result," Keynes (1936, pp. 82–83) continues, "are just as genuine as any other savings. No one can be compelled to own the additional money corresponding to the new bank credit, unless he deliberately prefers to hold more money rather than some other form of wealth. Yet employment, incomes and prices cannot help moving in such a way that in the new situation someone does choose to hold the additional money." The creation of new money by the banks in order to finance investment expenditure will generate, in the hands of the ultimate holders of it as it is circulated through the real markets of the economy, what Basil Moore (1988, passim) in an insightful analysis has referred to as "convenience lending" and what I shall refer to in a related context later, following the terminology that Keynes has just adopted, as *convenience saving*.

That the earlier literature had understood money as substantially a veil does not need any extensive explanation. Schumpeter has addressed the point eloquently. Drawing a distinction between real analysis and monetary analysis, he observed that the period that followed the developments in the theory of money in the eighteenth century witnessed "a victory of Real Analysis that was so complete as to put Monetary Analysis practically out of court for well over a century" (Schumpeter, 1954, p. 282; see also Vickers, 1975). It is not true, of course, that there had been no work, or no important work, in monetary analysis during the classical period. Jacob Hollander (1911), Richard Sayers (1953), Jacob Viner (1937), and John Hicks (1967), among others, have thrown important light on the topic. Viner's classic examination of the bullionist controversies of the early nineteenth century continues to warrant careful attention, and his discussion of the currency school and the banking school positions are relevant to the question of the exogeneity or the endogeneity of the money supply that I will take up again later. Hicks's (1967, ch. 10) discussion of Henry Thornton's well-known *Paper Credit* has emphasized the extent to which that early work addressed many Keynesian questions and other more modern issues.

But the good deal of work on monetary affairs, including the large amount of what Keynes, following his *Treatise*, allowed to "fall into the background" as "technical monetary detail" (1936, p. vii), does not obscure the fact that nineteenth-century economists did, by and large, hold to the view that the analysis of the economic system could be dichotomized into that of a real sector and a monetary sector. The distinction between what Schumpeter characterized as real and monetary analysis was taken up by Patinkin (1965), who examined the invalid dichotomy issue in neoclassical theory. His argument has been further evaluated by Rogers (1989) in his important *Money, Interest and Capital*, in a manner that is relevant to our present investigation. John Stuart Mill, notwithstanding some highly suggestive arguments to the contrary in his *Essays on Some Unsettled Questions*, concluded that "there cannot, in short, be intrinsically a more insignificant thing, in the economy of society, than money . . . .It is a machine for doing quickly and commodiously, what would be done, though less quickly and commodiously, without i t. . . .It only exerts a distinct and independent influence of its own when it gets out of order" (1909, p. 488). The brilliance of Mill's conclusion, however, is not in his view of money as a veil, or, as Pigou (1941; excerpted in Clower, 1970, p. 34) early in the twentieth century called it, a "garment or a wrapper" over economic affairs. It is in his recognition that money does "get out of order" and that it is then that many aspects of its true significance emerge in full light. One senses an anticipation of Hyman Minsky's (1982) perception of the endogenously generated cyclical instability that is characteristic of a monetary market economy.

Wicksell discussed at length the cyclical instabilities induced by the divergence of money market or nominal rates of interest from what he saw as natural rates. That discussion might appear to place him in the camp of monetary rather than real analysts. But he must nevertheless be understood as falling under the latter heading. This follows from his insistence that the natural rate of interest, which functioned in many respects as what the present day neo-Ricardians see as a center of gravitation of the system, is explicable by reference to real causes—namely, the real marginal productivity of the economy's capital stock.[3] The other main component of neoclassical and contemporary analysis—the neo-Walrasian scheme—essentially sees no need for money at all. The point has been discussed expansively by Davidson (1978) and numerous authors whose analysis adopts a Post-Keynesian perspective (see Vickers, 1985). Frank Hahn (1970) also has concluded that "the Walrasian economy. . . is essentially one of barter (Davidson, 1979, p. xiii). From this perspective Hahn has spoken further of the inessential nature of money and has explained that "the main content of the monetary theory of an inessential economy is implicit in its construction: there is nothing we can say about the equilibrium of an economy with 'money' that one cannot say about the equilibrium of a non-monetary economy" (1973, p. 231; see Rogers, 1989, p. 46).

What the classical and the neoclassical theories point to, and what characterizes much of contemporary analysis such as the new classical economics with its reliance on rational expectations and infinite market-clearing velocities, is the neutrality of money. Money is neutral, we can say, if changes in the quantity of money in circulation do not cause any change in the equilibrium solution values of such real variables as the level of output, employment, relative commodity prices, and the real rate of interest. In that case its only effect is to cause a proportional change in the absolute money price level. The analytical system is thereby completely dichotomized. In many expressions of the neoclassical analysis it is acknowledged that though money might well be nonneutral in the short run, neutrality obtains in the long run (though the rational expectations, policy irrelevance theorem concludes that money is neutral in both the short run and the long run).

Our immediate concern, to the contrary, is with the manner in which the existence and circulation of money affect the operation of the aggregate system in an essential way, in both the short run and the longer run. On the level of the individual firm—for example, in relation to optimal operating levels, factor combinations, investment expenditures, and capital expansion—the monetary and financial aspects of relevant decisions need to be taken clearly into account. On the aggregate level, such decision problems and outcomes find an analog in the provision of finance that is necessary to facilitate an expansion of investment. That, as can be seen from the quotations earlier, is the precise issue that Keynes addressed.

Most pointedly, the question arises, in the context of expanded investment and capital formation, "Where does the money come from?" Can or does saving finance investment? If the classical conception of Say's law could be shown to have validity, then saving flows into and finances investment. This is, no doubt, the notion behind the Turgot-Smith savings-investment doctrine (see Schumpeter, 1954, p. 324), which sees an automatic mechanism that transforms saving into investment. It also lies behind the Ricardian notion of the progress of the economy toward the stationary state as the investment of the savings out of capitalists' profits propels the system forward. At the same time, a declining rate of profit on capital investment is induced by the pressure of diminishing marginal productivity in the wage good industries, notably agriculture. That puts an upward pressure on the money wage rate and causes a decline in the profit rate. But clearly, more is involved than the notion, as the classical analysis saw it, of such an automaticity in the savings and investment flows. For if it is true, as the

Keynesian multiplier analysis has led us to believe, that the causal relation needs to be reversed and that it is investment that generates saving, the question arises as to how the saving, which comes later in real time than the investment, can provide the finance, or the expendable funds, to make that investment possible. What, in short, are the savings that investment expenditures generate? What processes of financial flows operate to bring investment and saving into equality with one another? What relations exist between the flows of values in the financial sector and the generation of values and, thereby, the motivation for economic activity, in the real sector? What interdependence exists, in other words, between market outcomes in the respective spheres of circulation?

4.2.

Consider, first, the firm's demand for money capital. A number of considerations on this level provide a background to the macroeconomics of money capital investment. An adequate foundation for our subsequent discussion can be provided by the following minimal observations. They address the fact that inadequacies of analysis at this point have caused a serious hiatus in the neoclassical theory of the firm and its optimizing behavior. Two important distinctions need to be borne in mind. First, analysis must focus on the distinction between the real capital and the money capital employed by the firm. The former, along with cooperating monetary and working capital assets such as inventories and accounts receivable, is described on the assets side of the firm's balance sheet. The latter is described on the liabilities side of the balance sheet that depicts in summary form the financing sources, or the sources of money capital, employed in the firm. Money capital is not to be understood as a factor of production. It describes, rather, the source and magnitude of the funds available to the firm to be used to finance the investment in real capital and other assets. Real capital, properly interpreted, is a factor of production. But in the context of a flow-flow production and factor use analysis, in which a flow of factor services is understood to provide a flow of product output, it is not the real capital asset—the machine tool, for example—that is to be understood as the factor of production. That productive factor is to be interpreted as the flow of services provided by the real capital asset.

Second, we are here speaking of the firm's demand for money capital. We are not yet speaking of its demand for money. The firm's demand for and use of money capital is depicted, as has been said, on the liabilities side of its balance sheet. That money capital, which will be obtained in general in the form of short-term loans, longer-term debt, and equity capital (including retained earnings), is invested by the firm in numerous possible ways, depending on decision preferences, optimization criteria, and expected future value realizations. One of the assets in which the money capital may be invested is money. To the extent that the firm allocates its available money capital to investment in money balances, it is to that extent satisfying its liquidity requirement, but it is thereby reducing the extent to which that money capital would otherwise be available for the financing of real capital assets and an expanded production process.[4]

The neoclassical theory of the firm has expanded, of course, beyond the immediate or short-run analysis in which day-to-day production and variable factor use decisions are made. But the attempts to accommodate analytically the use of fixed or real capital assets have not in general achieved a satisfying integration of the real and the financial theories and decision problems of the firm. The real and the financial theories of the firm have followed separate and unsymbiotic developments. No satisfactory recognition has been given, moreover, to the problems that arise when account is taken of the uncertainties and the essential ignorance of the future, in the context of which decisions in the firm are necessarily made.[5]

Earlier analysis of the manner in which the conventional theory of the firm is in need of amendment to take account of its money capital financing problem makes extended discussion at this point unnecessary (see Davidson, 1978, p. xii). It has been shown that the traditional conceptions of marginal optimization and the relevant factor use decisions do not get at the heart of the relations that exist between the firm's real and financial decisions and their bearing on its optimum structure and operations. For implicit in the conventional neoclassical procedure is the assumption that the firm exists and operates in what we may refer to as a condition of money capital saturation. By this term we refer to the fact, or the supposition, that the firm has ready access at all times to as much money capital as it needs in order to enable it to operate at any desired level of output, with any desired quantity or combination of factor inputs. In fact, however, account needs to be taken of the manner in which the firm's structural and operating decisions are subject to what we have referred to previously as a money capital availability constraint (see Vickers, 1968).

When account is taken of the pressure and the significance of that constraint, it becomes clear that money capital financing costs must be imputed to factors of production. It follows that decisions as to the firm's optimum or desirable operating structure will be influenced by what we have termed the *money capital intensity of the factors*. This refers to the amount of money capital that must be introduced to the firm in order to provide for the presence of each unit of factor services.

Leaving aside for the present the fuller analysis of the interconnections between the firm's financing and factor use decisions, it follows that what must come to prominence for our present purposes is the effective cost to the firm of introducing additional money capital—or, as has been said, of relaxing the money capital-availability constraint. For that, effective cost provides the benchmark for incremental capital-investment decisions. If the firm obtains new money capital by selling a new issue of debt securities, it becomes necessary to specify appropriately the full marginal cost of debt capital. It is similarly necessary, under relevant conditions, to specify the full marginal cost of equity capital. In any event, the cost of money capital that is relevant to investment and financing decisions at the level of the firm and that lies behind the following analysis is to be understood as the appropriately specified, full marginal cost of relaxing the money capital–availability constraint (Vickers, 1987a).

4.3.

A valid insight implicit in the foregoing analysis provides a point of entry to the Post-Keynesian theory of the firm and its financial market dependence. This does not depend on what would be the untenable assumption that, in the uncertainties that abound in the real world, it is possible to conceive of stable and well-defined behavior functions and relations such as conventional analysis may suggest. The parametric forms of behavior functions cannot be specified independently of the passing and the pressures of real time and history. Rather, the usefulness of a reconstructed analysis rests in its ability to alert us to the nature of the causation and the directions of relationships that subsist and that demand recognition for decision purposes. Though stable functions and curves do not exist over real time in real-world economies, it is a valid insight that in the decision about the worthwhileness of expanded capital investment, for example, attention must be paid to the possible increase in the value of the firm that may result from it, and to the effective cost, at the margin of decision, of the money capital that is necessary to finance the investment.

Thus, there enters the analysis, as a basic building block of the Post-Keynesian theory, the Keynesian concept of the marginal efficiency of investment. This points to a decision criterion that conceives of the economic value of capital expenditure as the increment to the value of the firm that results from discounting the incremental income stream that can be expected to result from the investment at a discount factor, or capitalization rate, specified by the best estimate of the firm's full marginal cost of relaxing the money capital availability constraint. That incremental economic value can then be compared with the supply price of the capital goods that must be acquired, plus the incremental investment in working capital assets associated with the new capital project.

It has been forcibly argued, by Pierangelo Garegnani, for example, that the notion of the marginal efficiency of capital is "the Achilles' heel" of Keynes's critique of the neoclassical theory (Garegnani, 1983, p. 60). John Eatwell also joins in the critique of the concept, arguing that it "was itself derived from the neoclassical schedule" (Eatwell and Milgate, 1983, p. 121). But such claims are not to the point. The concept does not require any surrender to the neoclassical notions of capital that were rebutted in the famous Cambridge critique of neoclassical capital theory (see Harcourt, 1972). That this is so has been clarified by Luigi Pasinetti and convincingly argued by Colin Rogers.[6]

Consider, then, that based on its estimate of the marginal efficiency of investment, and incorporating in its decision process an estimate of the relevant marginal cost of money capital, the firm decides to undertake investment expenditure. The question arises as to how that investment expenditure is to be financed. It has frequently been observed that a large part of such industrial expenditures is made out of firms' accumulated retained earnings. The fact is well substantiated. But it is an analytical superficiality to leave the matter at that point. To the extent that the net earnings of previous periods have been retained in the firm rather than distributed to the owners in the form of dividends, the relevant amounts will have been reflected on the liabilities side of the firm's balance sheet as additions to the equity capital employed in the firm. But what must be considered is the precise use to which the cash-flow counterpart of the retained earnings has been put. To the extent that earnings have been retained, to that extent a part of the net periodic cash flow generated by the firm's production activities and sales will have been retained. The cash may have been put to various uses. It may have been used to repay short-term loans or retire long-term debt. In that case the firm's debt-to-equity financing ratio would have been changed. The cash may have been held in bank balances or invested in marketable securities as part of the management of the firm's liquid asset position. Or it may already have been invested in fixed capital assets of one kind or another.

For investment to proceed, it is necessary to consider not simply the extent to which retained earnings may have increased the firm's equity position in the past, but whether there is immediately available in the firm an amount of cash sufficient to finance the investment expenditure. In short, the immediate source of finance will be either immediately available cash, the proceeds of the sale of marketable securities, both of which will have been recorded on the assets side of the balance sheet, or new borrowings from one or more of several financial intermediaries. To the extent that previously held cash is used, there will, of course, be no increase in the money supply as a result of the investment expenditure, but the transformation of previously idle into active balances might be interpreted as an increase in the velocity of circulation of money. We shall return to the point. To the extent that industrial firms sell part of their holdings of marketable securities to nonbank investors or speculators in order to provide finance for the investment expenditure, such sales, depending on the extent to which in the aggregate economy they occur, will put pressure on security prices and imply a tendency for security yields and market rates of interest to increase. That, in turn, will imply an upward pressure on what we have already inspected as the cost of money capital and may thereby moderate the aggregate level of investment that would otherwise occur. In that case again, money is being enticed out of idle or speculative balances into active circulation and no increase in the money supply occurs.

What is at issue here is the relation between the real multiplier effects of investment expenditures and the associated effects and disturbances in the financial sector. Dennis Robertson, at whose time-period analysis we shall look again in the following section, has referred to Kahn's observation, in his initial introduction of the multiplier concept, that "I am here considering the position in the final position of equilibrium when everything has settled down.... I do not enter into the question of [the] time lag." Robertson (1940, pp. 11–118) observes that "if, with Mr. Kahn, we are prepared to forget about the period of transition, we can declare the problem of the finance of the process of investment to be self-solving."[7] But such an analytical luxury is not, in fact, available to us.

In the general case, industrial firms will finance investment expenditures by taking, in the short term, increased bank loans. This is possible by virtue of the fact that industrial corporations frequently, if not generally, maintain arrangements with banks that permit them to draw as required against established lines of credit. They form part of what Hicks has referred to as the overdraft sector (Hicks, 1974, p. 51). This increased demand for money, or what Keynes came to see as the coping stone of his liquidity preference theory, has been referred to as the finance demand (see Davidson, 1978, pp. 159–162). Keynes saw, as instanced in the references to his post–*General Theory* writing that we noted at the beginning, that it was this demand for short-term cash accommodation that made the expansion possible. "Credit expansion," he argued, "provides not an alternative to increased saving, but a necessary preparation for it. It is the parent, not the twin, of increased saving" (Keynes, 1939, p. 572, quoted in Kregel, 1984–1985, p. 151).

The fact that the banks in this way increase their loan advances against industrial lines of credit means that the money supply increases in response to the demand for it. The money supply is thereby endogenous. The expenditure of the newly created money means that it passes into the hands of the suppliers of the factors of production that are activated by the increased investment expenditure. It passes through the hands of the capital goods-producing firms, into the hands of materials suppliers, to workers' bank balances, and thereby to either consumption expenditures or liquid asset holdings. The money begins a journey of active circulation. Thence, as Robertson observed, "All the money that is anywhere must be somewhere" (1959, p. 125, quoted in Kregel, 1986, p. 95). The important question at issue, however, is that of the use that is made of the increased money supply by its successive recipients.

When a firm makes an investment-expenditure commitment and concludes the necessary short-term financing arrangements, it will at the same time anticipate that in due course it will sell long-term securities in the money capital market and that with the proceeds of such a sale it will retire its short-term bank loans. That long-term capital may be obtained, as we have seen, in the form of debt capital or equity capital. In either case, the services of an investment banker will be retained to market the long-term securities. The investment banker is said to underwrite the new capital issue, meaning that he agrees to purchase the new issue from the firm and, hopefully, resell it to investors or speculators in the capital market. The investment banker will frequently hedge his position by subcontracting part of the new issue to subunderwriters, such as other financial intermediary institutions and pension funds. But the issuing firm will have made its investment-expenditure decision on the basis of its estimate of its cost of capital, implying that it plans or hopes to sell its new long-term security at a price implicit in its cost-of-capital estimate. Whether that can in due course be done depends on the investment banking commitments it is able to secure, and possibly on money capital market conditions at the time the new issue comes to market. The timing, estimates, and anticipation of financial market conditions are therefore acutely relevant and important.

It is to be noted that all of these arrangements and procedures occur without any person's prior commitment of savings, and before the savings that will result from the income expansion induced by the investment expenditure will have occurred. Investment precedes saving in causation and in time. Whether, in due course, the long-term, capital security issue can be floated in the capital market at the hoped for price, or at the initially projected yield or effective interest rate, will depend on the savings funds that are made available by the recipients of the higher induced incomes. Davidson (1986) has analyzed the relevant financial flows in some detail and has observed that the likelihood of floating the new capital issue at previously anticipated prices and yields depends on what he calls the marginal propensity of income earners to purchase securities out of saving. If security market conditions make it necessary to discount the new issue price further than had been anticipated, that will imply an increase in the effective yield or interest rate, with possibly negative effects on further investment expenditures.

From this analysis of the financing of investment expenditure and its induced and lagged effects, it is possible to draw a number of summary conclusions. First, much depends, for the outcome and effects in the financial as distinct from the real markets, on the precise structure of the channels of financial flows and the institutional framework within which the system functions. Operatively relevant is what has been termed the degree and structure of financial intermediation that exists. Kaldor (1960) made much of the point in his stimulating discussion of "speculation and economic stability," and Minsky (1982, pp. 61–62), in numerous extended works, has expanded the analysis of the topic.

Second, the financial flows and their market impact are dependent in an acute sense on the decision of successive income recipients on two levels. The outcomes depend, on the one hand, on the marginal consumption propensities that are operative and, on the other hand, on the public's decision as to the forms in which savings are to be held. The implied forces on both of these levels will determine the strength of the demands for capital securities of different kinds and different maturities, with the implied effects I have already noted for security prices and yields. The theory and analysis of individual and institutional asset portfolio structures thus gain significant relevance at this point.

Third, as we shall examine more fully in the next section, the demand for money can be expected in the general case to increase, not only for the purpose of the immediate financing of investment expenditures such as we have already examined, but also for normal transactions purposes. This will follow from the higher levels of economic activity and income generation that are induced. At that point the trading and payments habits of the public become relevant for their impact on the efficiency of money use or, in familiar terms, the velocity of circulation of money. That velocity may well increase if, in the industrial sector, business firms react to any increase in interest rates by managing their operating cash balances more efficiently. Or it may be conceived to increase as idle balances are transformed into active balances, as the edging upward of interest rates and yields pry speculative cash balances loose.

Fourth, the rate of realization of the real multiplier effects that follow from investment expansion will depend on the extent to which expansion in the consumption goods trades is anticipated or foreseen. If that foresight were perfect and complete, the multiplier effects would be realized more rapidly, or might hold more nearly instantaneously at all points in time. But the time lapse and the imperfection of expectations are again highly relevant. What occurs, therefore, as the interactions are in process between developments in the financial and the real sectors of the economy, is a changing structure of market prices and traded quantities. Inherent in the foregoing analysis is the recognition of prices, and the interrelations between prices, on a number of levels: first, consumption goods prices that are relevant to the consumption-saving decision; second, the supply prices of new capital goods that influence the worthwhileness at the margin of new capital investment expenditures; third, the prices of existing capital asset securities, implying market yields on existing industrial securities and thereby the estimates of the firm's cost of money capital; and fourth, the variable factor costs, notably the cost of labor expressed in the going money wage rate. It might be added that the conjunction between these prices, and the activity levels they collectively vindicate, determine the ongoing valuation of the firm, or the value of the capital goods currently in place and engaged in production. This implied market value of the firm's existing assets, reflected in the financial market's valuation of the firm's capital securities, may be used as an investment decision criterion, as in Tobin's famous q theory of investment.[8]

Fifth, it follows that the effective constraint on increased investment expenditure is a financial constraint. It is not true to say that savings constrains investment. The extent to which investment can proceed and can act to generate increased incomes and saving depends on the ability and the willingness of the banks to increase the money supply in response to the demand for it. It is necessary, of course, for the banks (and the other depository or money-creating institutions as defined in the Depository Institutions Deregulation and Monetary Control Act of 1980) to hold reserves, principally in the form of deposits at the Federal Reserve Bank, equal to no less than a stipulated percentage of their deposit liabilities. As the banks expand their loans and deposits, and thus the money supply, they must have reason to believe that the central bank will, in fact, take whatever action is necessary to supply reserves as they become necessary to support the deposits outstanding. That, however, is precisely the manner in which, in the contemporary monetary and market system, the banking relations operate. The principal function of the central bank is to act as the lender of last resort and thereby to guarantee the liquidity of the system. It is a mistaken vision of bank operations to imagine that the banks' deposit creation is ultimately constrained by their possession of reserves. Rather, the creation of bank reserves as that is rendered necessary by real activity developments in the economy follows the emergence of the banking system's need for reserves. That necessary creation of reserves is effected by the central bank's open market purchases of securities.

Sixth, this recognition that the money supply is therefore endogenous means that its supply is, in general, highly elastic. But it is elastic at a loan interest rate that is set by the banks at a mark-up above the exogenous rate at which the central bank is prepared to make reserves available. That rate recognizes, in general, the existing structure of open market rates, as well as international interest rates and the likelihood that either desired or unwanted money capital flows may result from international interest rate differentials. The central bank will and does, therefore, set its own lending rate at different policy-determined levels, influencing thereby the readiness with which liquidity is available or can be created within the financial sector.[9]

Seventh, a clear relation has emerged between the rates of return that, it is anticipated, can be generated on capital investment in real-sector activities and the rate of interest or the cost of money capital. But as a matter of doctrine, the relation between the one and the other, the marginal efficiency of capital and the rate of interest, is to be seen somewhat differently from the manner in which it was frequently perceived in the neoclassical scheme. For Wicksell, for example, the natural rate (the rate of interest that would equate saving and investment at full employment) was the center of gravitation of the system. The induced cyclical fluctuations in activity and prices (and the implied pressure on bank reserves) that resulted from a divergence of the market from the natural rate was conceived to bring the market rate of interest into line with the real or natural rate. For Keynes, on the other hand, and for the line of analysis I have adopted, it is the exogenously determined nominal or market rate that is the center of gravitation. The level of that rate determines, or anchors, the rate at which money capital is available to investing firms, and it therefore determines the level of the marginal efficiency of capital at which investment becomes, or ceases to be, economically worthwhile. Keynes, in other words, has reversed the relation between the marginal efficiency of capital and the rate of interest as the neoclassical scheme perceived it.

Finally, it can be noted that the new money supply that is created at the beginning of the investment process circulates and may find its way back to the banks. We have noted that in the process some of that incremental money supply may be absorbed as transactions balances that are necessary to support the new, higher level of economic and real market activity. Such increased demands will, themselves, put upward pressure on the rate of interest. But to the extent that the money supply returns to the banks— to the extent, for example, that it is regathered by the banks as the short-term borrowers repay bank loans, there is a temporary reduction of the money supply. Loans create deposits, and the repayment of loans destroys deposits. When that occurs, the banks are again in a position to extend loans to new borrowers, and there is active in the financial system what might be termed a revolving fund of finance. In short, the ability and readiness of the banks to continue to accommodate the economy's demand for money will depend on the banks' own liquidity preferences and their expectations of borrowers' profitability and income-generating prospects. It was for that reason that Keynes highlighted, as we saw at the beginning, the fact that "the banks hold the key position in the transition from a lower to a higher scale of activity."

4.4.

The foregoing analysis of mutually dependent real- and financial-sector developments makes it necessary to inspect more closely the generation of saving and its relation to the creation of money and the multiplier effects. In view of the time lags we have already taken somewhat into account, notably in the temporary financing of expenditures, it will be useful to explore the saving and money-creation effects with the aid of a simple time-period model, similar to that made famous at an earlier stage by Robertson (1940) in his discussions with Keynes. The upshot of the argument will be to the effect that the new money supplies that find their way into the hands of income earners after being spent by borrowers for investment purposes will represent immediate, though possibly temporary, convenience saving. To construct a simple model of income generation adequate to illustrate the points at issue, consider the following relations:

$$C_t = a + bY_{t-1}, \tag{4.1}$$

$$I_t = \overline{I}, \tag{4.2}$$

$$Y_t = C_t + I_t. \tag{4.3}$$

Voluntary savings, referred to as S_{vol} appear as

$$S_{vol} = Y_{t-1} - C_t = -a + (1 - b)Y_{t-1}. \tag{4.4}$$

Investment expenditure is for the moment taken to be autonomous, and consumption expenditure in any time period is dependent on income earned in the preceding period, with a marginal consumption propensity of b. Taking the sum of autonomous expenditure components as defined by $a + I = A$, the path of the periodic income realizations is described by the first-order difference equation

$$Y_t - bY_{t-1} = A. \tag{4.5}$$

By usual solution methods the periodic income path is describable as

$$Y_t = \overline{\frac{A}{1-b}} + (Y_0 - \overline{\frac{A}{1-b}})b^t. \tag{4.6}$$

The data shown in Table 4.1 are based on the assumption that $C_t = 0.9Y_{t-1}$, and that periodic series for investment, consumption, income, and voluntary savings are recorded. The second to last column of the table records the periodic change in voluntary saving, which will be subject to further comment later. The final column records the actual saving, $S_t = Y_t - C_t$. The specimen data can be shown to be consistent with equation (4.6) by substitution, for any selected period, of the base period's values and the marginal consumption parameter. The table introduces the assumption, which will be commented on again later, that the level of investment expenditure increases permanently by 50 in the first period following the base period. Consistent with the traditional multiplier concepts, the ultimate increment in voluntary saving is the sum of a geometric series

TABLE 4.1

t	I	C	Increase in Y	S_{vol}	S_{vol}	S_t
0	100	900.00	1,000.00	100.00	—	100
1	150	900.00	1,050.00	100.00	—	150
2	150	945.00	1,095.00	105.00	5.00	150
3	150	985.50	1,135.50	109.50	4.50	150
4	150	1,021.95	1,171.95	113.55	4.05	150
Limit Values	150	1,350.00	1,500.00	150.00	—	150

commencing at the magnitude 5 and increasing by a factor of 0.9, which is equal to the marginal consumption propensity assumed in the table. This follows from the fact that the increase each period in voluntary saving can be shown to be defined as (1 - b), or one minus the consumption propensity, times the increase in income that occurred in the preceding period. That, in turn, is equal to the consumption propensity times the increase in income in the period before that. The voluntary saving is thus raised in the limit by 50 or by the same amount as the investment expenditure that instigated the multiplier process.

Of immediate interest, however, consistent with the analysis of the financing of incremental expenditures in the preceding section, is the question as to how the expenditure streams in this case are actually financed. Where, again, does the money come from?

Clearly, the increase in investment expenditure that instigates the multiplier process occurs before the voluntary savings that will ultimately be generated by it can be realized. Again we conclude that the investment is not, and cannot be, financed initially by saving. Again, therefore, an increase in the money supply is required to finance the process. With this in view, Table 4.2 recognizes that in the case being considered the increased money expenditure will accrue as income in the hands of income earners, but as their consumption expenditures are not influenced by it, those consumption expenditures being assumedly dependent on the preceding period's income, the increments of income will be recorded as what we now refer to as convenience saving, using the symbol S_{con} to describe the corresponding amount.

Table 4.2 indicates the periodic increases in the money supply that will be necessary to fill the gap between the projected levels of investment expen-

TABLE 4.2

		Increase in		
t	S_{vol}	M^s	S_{con}	S_t
0	100.0	—	—	100
1	100.0	25.000	50.0	150
2	105.0	22.500	45.0	150
3	109.5	20.250	40.5	150
4	113.5	18.225	36.5	150

diture and the voluntary saving that will be forthcoming under the assumed conditions. It will be noted that because the investment expenditure is assumed to be maintained at the new higher level to which it was raised in the first period, there will be a need for new money creation in each of the succeeding periods. This assumes, of course, that, in line with the fuller discussion in the preceding section, no money is attracted to the transactions sphere from idle balances, no change occurs in the rate of interest to make that desirable, and in other words, no change occurs in the velocity of circulation of money. The possible impact on the velocity of circulation will be considered later.

To provide a linkage with earlier literature, it is assumed in the argument as summarized in Table 4.2 that the structure-of-payments habits in the system is such that the money supply turns over twice during each time period and that incremental investment expenditures are implemented at a corresponding rate. The velocity of circulation of money is, therefore, 2. In that case, it is understood that the increase in the money supply necessary to finance the periodic increase in expenditure will be one-half that latter amount.[10] It is noted that the convenience saving for each period is twice the amount of the increase in the money supply, consistent with the assumption that the rate of turnover of the money supply remains constant at 2. Noticeably, the money supply will need to increase at a decreasing rate as the expansion proceeds. Summing the relevant geometric series, it can be shown that, in the limit, the money supply will increase in this case by 250, or by one-half of the increase in income. It will be seen also that the convenience saving tapers off at the same rate as the voluntary saving is increasing.

The data as constructed in the tables are consistent with and explain Robertson's observation in reference to this kind of situation, in which the multiplier-money supply interaction is brought into view, that "in each period the Authority is conceived of as acting only partly (and decreasingly) by increasing the supply of money, partly (and increasingly) by maintaining the income velocity of the previously issued supply" (1940, p. 118). The dynamics of the situation we have envisaged permit us to make a number of relevant analytical conclusions.

4.5.

The tables and the illustrative data in the preceding section, together with the difference equation model into which Robertson's earlier suggestions have been cast, are, of course, highly schematic. They do, however, emphasize a number of relevant issues. First, it should be understood that the velocity of circulation of money does not have, in the Post-Keynesian theory, the causative significance attributed to it in the earlier neoclassical analysis. It serves legitimately only as an ex post datum descriptive of realized outcomes. Its explanatory, or predictive, significance has been seriously misconceived by virtue of its appearance in the traditional quantity equation of exchange. Our analysis has emphasized consistently the activity-forming and the price-forming significance of expenditure decisions. The endogeneity of money, as we have exhibited it, implies forcibly that, as to the price-level relation that is generally embedded in the quantity theory, the causal relation, in fact, is not from the money supply to the price level but from the price level to the money supply. The money supply, we have seen, is created endogenously by the banks in response to the demand for it, as that demand is dependent, in turn, on the price level at which production and activity is conducted. That price level will depend on the cost pressures inherent in factor-use decisions and the mark-up that firms, depending on their perception of their market power, choose, or attempt, to adopt. The ability and willingness of the banks to expand the money supply, and the price or interest rate at which they do so, has been seen to depend on the decisions of the central bank to make reserves available to vindicate the increased money supply.

Second, it is to be expected that, in the kind of expansion process envisaged, the velocity of circulation may, in fact, be highly variable. This may be expected to follow for a number of reasons. Any possible change in the banks' desired liquidity position may cause their lending rate to edge upward as the borrowing to finance investment expenditure increases, particularly if increases in risk exposure are associated with the increased borrowing. This may, in turn, lift the general level of interest rates in the money market, inducing a change in individuals' liquidity preference and changes in their desired portfolios. As a result, the extent to which money might be shaken loose from previously held speculative balances will affect the effective velocity of circulation. At the same time, the monetary authorities may alter the interest rate at which they are willing to supply reserves to the banks to permit them to finance the expansion, and such policy-induced pressure on the market interest-rate structure can be expected to spill over to variations in the public's liquidity preference and the effective velocity of circulation of money.

Third, there is no reason to believe that as the expansion proceeds the consumption and savings propensities will remain constant at the assumed levels. Relevant, therefore, is the manner in which a change in the economy's saving rate will affect the flow of funds into the long-term capital market. In particular, changes may occur in the savers' propensity to allocate saving to the purchase of the long-term capital securities, which, we saw in the preceding section, would, in due course, be issued by the firms to retire, or fund, their temporary short-term borrowing that had facilitated the expansion. At the same time, there is no reason to believe that the time lags in expenditure and financing decisions would, in fact, be precisely those I have assumed for illustrative purposes.

Fourth, it should be borne in mind that not only will the possible variations I have just referred to affect the structure of prices and yields, or the effective interest rates, in the money and capital markets, but they will also have an impact on price levels in the real markets. I noted previously that such effects were to be expected in the consumption goods, the capital goods, and the labor markets. The impact of the expansion on the price dimension and the output dimension of national income, respectively, are not illustrated in the analysis I have constructed. The elaboration of such differential effects, the lack of which remains one of the more serious defects of the neoclassical scheme of things, has only lately benefitted from the Post-Keynesian developments (see Davidson, 1978; Vickers, 1987b).

Fifth, it can be seen that high degrees of interaction and criss-crossing of effects occur between the public's asset portfolio preferences and decisions, the similar preferences and decisions of the banks and the nonbank financial intermediaries that participate in the process, and the policy-determined actions of the central bank functioning in its capacity as the lender of last resort.

Finally, I have not yet addressed directly the manner in which all of the decisions and effects brought into view are influenced by the realities of uncertainty, ignorance, and the pressures on decisions and outcomes of the passing of real historical time. Progress has lately been made in analyses addressed to these questions, and significant work has appeared emanating from the perspectives that Shackle (1969), for example, has proposed (see also Vickers, 1987a; Katner, 1986, 1989–1990). But in the flux and the flow of real-world economic affairs, it is possible to see the general nature of what Keynes (1936, p. vii) referred to as the "dynamic development . . . the forces which determine changes in the scale of output and employment as a whole; and . . . [the fact that] . . . money enters into the economic scheme in an essential and peculiar manner." In the world as it exists, and in the analysis directed to the explanation of it, the monetary and the real are intricately interintrusive. Money matters. The supposition of its neutrality, in either the short run or the long run, is not analytically sustainable.

NOTES

1. Schumpeter (1954, p. 529) refers to Mill's *Essays* as "containing his freshest and most original contributions to economics."

2. Many of the relevant issues have been raised in a series of articles that stemmed from Asimakopulos (1983). See also Asimakopulos (1986), Kregel (1984–1985, 1986), Davidson (1986), and Snippe (1985). The classic discussions of the relation between the Keynesian multiplier and the velocity of circulation of money, to which reference will be made below, are contained in Lutz (1955), Archibald (1956), Tsiang (1956), and Wells (1971).

3. See Wicksell (1935, vol. 2, pp. 27, 188, 194, 215). See also Rogers (1989) for an expanded evaluation of Wicksell, notably in relation to the results of the Cambridge critique in the theory of capital. The neo-Ricardian center of gravitation notion is advanced in Eatwell and Milgate (1983) and Milgate (1982).

4. The following is heavily indebted to earlier and more extended analysis contained in Vickers (1968, 1970, 1987a, 1987b, 1989).

5. An important advance toward the remedy of this analytical deficiency has recently seen made by Katzner (1990).

6. See also the insightful conclusions of Pasinetti (1974, p. 43) quoted in Rogers (1989, p. 170). See also Schumpeter (1954, p. 1119n).

7. Robertson's emphasis on the transition recalls Keynes's observation that "it is in the transition [from a lower to a higher scale of economic activity] that we actually have our being" (1936, p. 343n).

8. For a relevant discussion see Crotty (1990) and the rejoinder by Tobin and Brainard (1990).

9. See Moore (1988) for an extended discussion of monetary endogeneity.

10. See the earlier explorations of the multiplier-money supply relation in Lutz (1955), Archibald (1956), Tsiang (1956), Wells (1971), and Chick (1973, 1983, ch. 14). See also Moore (1988, p. 340).

REFERENCES

Archibald, G. C. (1956). "Multiplier and Velocity Analysis: An Annulment." *Economica*, 23 (91), 265–269.

Asimakopulos, A. (1983). "Kalecki and Keynes on Finance, Investment and Saving." *Cambridge Journal of Economics*, 7, 221–233.

———. (1986). "Finance, Liquidity, Saving and Investment." *Journal of Post Keynesian Economics*, 9, 79–90.

Chick, V. (1973). "Financial Counterparts of Saving and Investment and Inconsistency in Some Simple Macro Models." *Weltwirtschaftliches Archiv*, 109, 621–643.

———. (1983). *Macroeconomics after Keynes: A Reconsideration of the General Theory*. Cambridge, MA: The MIT Press.

Clower, R. W. (Ed.). (1970). *Monetary Theory*. London: Penguin.

Crotty, J. R. (1990). "Owner-Manager Conflict and Financial Theories of Investment Instability: A Critical Assessment of Keynes, Tobin, and Minsky." *Journal of Post Keynesian Economics*, 12, 519–542.

Davidson, P. (1978). *Money and the Real World* (2nd ed.). New York: Wiley.

———. (1986). "Finance, Funding, Saving, and Investment." *Journal of Post Keynesian Economics*, 9, 101–110.

Eatwell, J., and M. Milgate. (Eds.). (1983). *Keynes's Economics and the Theory of Value and Distribution*. New York: Oxford University Press.

Garegnani, P. (1983). "Notes on Consumption, Investment and Effective Demand." In J. Eatwell and M. Milgate (Eds). *Keynes's Economics and the Theory of Value and Distribution*. New York: Oxford University Press.

Hahn, F. H. (1970). "Some Adjustment Problems." *Econometrica*.

———. (1973). "On the Foundations of Monetary Theory." In M. Parker (Ed.). *Essays on Modern Economics*. London: Longmans.

Harcourt, G. C. (1972). *Some Cambridge Controversies in the Theory of Capital*. Cambridge: Cambridge University Press.

Hicks, J. (1967). *Critical Essays in Monetary Theory*. Clarendon Press.

———. (1974). *The Crisis in Keynesian Economics*. Oxford: Blackwell.

Hollander, J. H. (1911). "The Development of the Theory of Money from Adam Smith to David Ricardo." *Quarterly Journal of Economics*, 25, 429–470.

Hutchison, T. W. (1988). *Before Adam Smith: The Emergence of Political Economy, 1662–1776*. Oxford: Blackwell.

Kaldor, N. (1939). "Speculation and Economic Stability." *Review of Economic Studies* (October). Originally published in 1939 in *Essays on Economic Stability and Growth*. Glencoe, IL: The Free Press of Glencoe.

Katzner, D. W. (1986). "Potential Surprise, Potential Confirmation and Probability." *Journal of Post Keynesian Economics*, 9, 58–78.

———.(1989–1990). "The Shackle-Vickers Approach to Decision-Making in Ignorance." *Journal of Post Keynesian Economics*, 12, 237–259.

———. (1990). "The Firm under Conditions of Ignorance and Historical Time." *Journal of Post Keynesian Economics*, 13, 125–145.

Keynes, J. M. (1936). *The General Theory of Employment, Interest, and Money*. London: Macmillan.

———. (1937a). "The Ex-Ante Theory of the Rate of Interest." *Economic Journal*, 47, 663–669.

———. (1937b). "Alternative Theories of the Rate of Interest." *Economic Journal*, 47, 241–252.

———. (1939). "The Process of Capital Formation." *Economic Journal*, 49, 569–574.

Kregel, J. A. (1984–1985). "Constraints on the Expansion of Output and Employment: Real or Monetary." *Journal of Post Keynesian Economics*, 7, 139–152.

———. (1986). "A Note on Finance, Liquidity, Saving and Investment." *Journal of Post Keynesian Economics*, 9, 91–100.

Lutz, V. (1955). "Multiplier and Velocity Analysis: A Marriage." *Economica* (February), 29–44.

Milgate, M. (1982). *Capital and Employment: A Study of Keynes's Economics*. London: Academic Press.

Mill, J. S. (1909). *Principles of Political Economy*. Edited by Sir W. J. Ashley. London: Longmans, Green. Originally published in 1848.

Minsky, H. P. (1982). *Can "It" Happen Again? Essays on Instability and Finance*. Armonk, NY: Sharpe.

Moore, B. J. (1988). *Horizontalists and Verticalists: The Macroeconomics of Credit Money*. Cambridge: Cambridge University Press.

Pasinetti, L. L. (1974). *Growth and Income Distribution: Essays in Economic Theory*. Cambridge: Cambridge University Press.

Patinkin, D. (1965). *Money, Interest, and Prices* (2nd Ed.). New York: Harper & Row.

Pigou, A. C. (1941). *The Veil of Money*. London: Macmillan.

Robertson, D. H. (1940). "Effective Demand and the Multiplier." In *Essays in Monetary Theory*. London: King.

———. (1959). *Money*. Cambridge: Cambridge University Press.

Rogers, C. (1989). *Money, Interest and Capital*. Cambridge: Cambridge University Press.

Sayers, R. S. (1953). "Ricardo's Views on Monetary Questions." In T. S. Ashton and R. S. Sayers (Eds.). *Papers in English Monetary History*. Oxford: Clarendon.

Schumpeter, J. A. (1954). *History of Economic Analysis*. New York: Oxford University Press.

Shackle, G. L. S. (1969). *Decision, Order, and Time in Human Affairs*. Cambridge: Cambridge University Press.

Silk, L. (1984). "Getting Back to the Real World." *Journal of Post Keynesian Economics*, 6, 483–485.

Snippe, J. (1985). "Finance, Saving and Investment in Keynes's Economics." *Cambridge Journal of Economics*, 9, 257–269.

Tobin, J., and W. Brainard. (1990). "On Crotty's critique of the q-Theory." *Journal of Post Keynesian Economics*, 12, 543–549.

Tsiang, S. C. (1956). "Liquidity Preference and Loanable Funds Theories, Multiplier and Velocity Analysis: A Synthesis." *American Economic Review*, 46, 539–564.

Vickers, D. (1959). *Studies in the Theory of Money, 1690–1776*. Philadelphia: Chilton.

———. (1968). *The Theory of the Firm: Production, Capital, and Finance*. New York: McGraw-Hill.

———. (1970). "The Cost of Capital and the Structure of the Firm." *Journal of Finance*, 25 (1), 35–46.

———. (1975). "Adam Smith and the Status of the Theory of Money." In A. S. Skinner and T. Wilson (Eds.). *Essays on Adam Smith*. Oxford: Clarendon Press.

———. (1985). "On Relational Structures and Non-Equilibrium in Economic Theory." *Eastern Economic Journal*, 11, 384–403.

———. (1987a). *Money Capital in the Theory of the Firm*. Cambridge: Cambridge University Press.

———.(1987b). "Aggregate Supply and the Producers' Expected Demand Curve: Performance and Change in the Macroeconomy." *Journal of Post Keynesian Economics*, 10, 84–104.

Viner, J. (1937). *Studies in the Theory of International Trade*. New York: Harper.

Wells, P. (1971). "Liquidity Preference and the Flow of Finance." *Journal of Money, Credit and Banking*, 3, 123–136.

Wicksell, K. (1935). *Lectures in Political Economy*, Vols. I and II. Edited by L. Robbins. London: Routledge and Kegan Paul.

5

MR. KEYNES, THE NEW KEYNESIANS, AND THE CONCEPT OF FULL EMPLOYMENT

WILLIAM DARITY, JR., AND ARTHUR H. GOLDSMITH

The debate in macroeconomics over the nature of full employment has centered on identification of the numerical value of the natural rate of unemployment. In short, at any point in time, what is the full employment unemployment rate? This necessarily has been construed as primarily an empirical task—sometimes involving the use of extremely sophisticated econometric techniques (for example, Salemi, 1991; Adams and Coe, 1990; and Salop, 1979)—but this investigation has proceeded as if there were no ambiguity about the concept of full employment itself or about the companion concept of the natural rate of unemployment.

Indeed, evidence of higher-than-customary rates of unemployment in the post–World War II era in the United States led to speculation that there was an upward drift in the natural rate of unemployment—that is, the full employment unemployment rate was becoming higher and higher. The standard explanations were alterations in the demographic composition of the labor force to include greater proportions of persons from groups of the population with weaker labor force attachments and the work disincentive effects of social insurance programs. Macrostabilization policy could not lower the rising "permanent" rate of unemployment, and, presumably, policymakers could not be expected to do much to lower prevailing unemployment rates since the full employment threshold was higher than it had been historically. Any steps that could be taken would have to alter the incentives confronting suppliers of labor rather than affect conditions of aggregate demand in the economy as a whole (Feldstein, 1973).

This position did not go unchallenged. In separate studies Cain (1979) and Summers (1986) showed that observed higher rates of unemployment could not be satisfactorily explained by demographic changes in the labor force, and Summers (1986) cast doubt on the significance of the adverse impact on labor supply of the existence of unemployment insurance. The thrust of these inquiries was to suggest that the economy generally was further away from the full employment unemployment rate than was supposed by the Feldsteinians and sustained a research momentum that continued to focus on the empirical issue of determining precisely what is the natural rate of unemployment. The concept of full employment, in and of itself, was not called into question.

Our purpose in this article is to demonstrate that there are profound difficulties with the idea of full employment as well as the idea of the natural rate of unemployment as construed customarily. We will show that these difficulties were present in the extensions and interpretations of Keynes's *General Theory* that emerged in the writings of Keynes's colleagues at Cambridge in the 1930s and that the surreptitious persistence of these difficulties has important and disturbing implications for the thrust of the New Keynesian research agenda as well as the legitimacy of the appellation Keynesian.

To illustrate our first point—that the notion of full employment has been problematic from the start of the Keynesian revolution—we examine in some detail two works of a pair of Keynes's disciples, his supervision pupil David Champernowne (1936) and perhaps his most famous standard bearer, Joan Robinson (1937).

Champernowne's essay, "Unemployment, Basic and Monetary," probably written before *The General Theory* appeared in print, although it was published shortly thereafter (Young, 1987), is especially notable for an interpretation of Keynes's argument in a fashion that would warm Milton Friedman's (1968) heart. According to Champernowne, the distinction that Keynes draws between his own views and those of the classical (whom Champernowne says are best represented by A. C. Pigou) is over the consequences of wage bargains. The classical/Marshallian/Pigovian school would have it that labor can determine its real wage via the wage bargaining process; Keynes has it that labor can determine its money wage only through the wage bargaining process. Keynes's claim will appear persuasive to some readers, observes Champernowne (1936, p. 201), only in the "short period of, say, one year"; it is "less convincing, when they refer to the effect of bargaining over a long stretch of years."

Champernowne (1936, p. 201) goes on to comment: "If labour is fundamentally discontented with its real wage year after year and is unsuccessful in raising it, some violent form of disequilibrium must arise which will eventually cause unemployment and induce labour to accept its real wage; if labour is so disorganised by unemployment that the competition of the unemployment continually lowers money wages, a situation must eventually arise in which the monetary authority takes action to check any resultant fall in prices, and so makes effective the attempt of the unemployed to accept a lower real wage."

In effect, Champernowne places the Pigovian or classical analysis in a chronological long period while Keynes's approach is placed in a chronological short period.[1] The wage bargain can only lead to a disequilibrium real wage in Champernowne's account in the chronological short period, a period of a year or so. Over the longer term labor's agreement to a reduction in the nominal wage must translate into a reduction in the real wage, if only because the monetary authorities will not allow the general price level to go into freefall.[2] At least of equal fundamental importance is Champernowne's implicit suggestion that over time labor will learn what type of real wage its money wage bargain will yield as it learns more about the progression of change in the general price level.

The distinction between long and short periods carries over to Champernowne's treatment of categories of unemployment, the line he draws been *basic* and *monetary* unemployment. First, he defines the notion of the basic real wage—the real wage that a laborer would demand if the cost of living had remained unchanged for a substantial period of time. That is to say, when laborers bargain for a particular money wage, they will know exactly what the real wage is they will receive, given the stationarity of the price level for the goods they purchase. Correspondingly, "basic unemployment" is "the amount of unemployment that would be in that situation if each man demanded neither more no less than his basic real wage" (Champernowne, 1936, p. 203).

In contrast, when the cost of living is not stationary, it is possible for laborers to err in seeking a particular real wage. They can miscalculate what the money wage will purchase when the price level is changing. If the cost of living is rising in a way that they do not anticipate fully, their real wage will be falling; and employers will be willing to hire more workers. The actual unemployment will be less than the basic unemployment. If the cost of living is falling in a way they do not anticipate fully, their real wage will be rising; and employers will be reluctant to hire more workers. Actual unemployment will exceed basic unemployment.

These latter two circumstances are disequilibrium conditions. In the case in which actual unemployment is above the basic level, Champernowne defines what he calls *monetary unemployment*, a case in which a rising real wage is above the basic real wage. The analysis closely parallels Milton Friedman's (1968) much later distinction between the short- and long-run expectations augmented Phillips curve. Friedman's short-run curve has its renowned negative slope because of real-wage miscalculations that keep the aggregate labor market from clearing. When the economy is moving rightward along a short-run Phillips curve, it would be experiencing Champernowne's monetary unemployment. On the other hand, the natural rate of unemployment associated with labor market clearing and the long-run (vertical) Phillips curve is exactly analogous to Champernowne's (1936, p. 204) basic unemployment:

> The unemployment rate of the monetary-unemployed is due to the fact that they, or their unions, have overlooked a recent fall in the cost-of-living, whereas employment of the monetary-employed is due to the fact that they have overlooked a rise in the cost-of-living. In so far as these oversights are likely to be repaired eventually, the monetary-unemployed are likely to lower the money-wage which they demand, and the monetary-employed are likely to raise the money wage-rate which they demand. We may express this by saying that a period of monetary employment is likely to cause rising money-wages. In so far as we can assume that rising and falling money-wages will respectively cause rising and falling real wages, we may conclude that a period of monetary employment contains the seeds of its own destruction in the form of a tendency for real wages to rise, whereas a period of monetary unemployment has in it the seeds of its own destruction, in the shape of a tendency for wages to fall.

This is suggestive of an eventual adjustment to basic unemployment—or to Friedman's natural rate of unemployment. But will a rise or fall of money wages necessarily mean a rise or fall of the real wage? Only, says Keynes, according to Champernowne, if the monetary authorities take the proper actions! Under laissez-faire there is no assurance that money-wage cuts will mean real wage cuts. If a reduction in money wages is agreed to by labor to ensure that the real wage falls, the monetary authorities would need to lower the rate of interest to make unemployment fall. The interest rate decline would, presumably, bolster aggregate demand via the investment channel and put upward pressure on the general price level: "the demand for labour for a certain real wage can only make itself effective in so far as it influences the attitude of the monetary authority and its manipulation of the rate of interest" (Champernowne, 1936, p. 204).

In Champernowne's view, the classical theory of unemployment is solely the theory of basic unemployment. Keynes's theory encompasses both basic and monetary unemployment.[3] Basic unemployment constitutes the reference point for full employment: "we may regard the trend value of unemployment as being equal to the level of basic unemployment since we may expect the actual level of unemployment to oscillate more or less regularly about the level of basic unemployment" (Champernowne, 1936, p. 206).

The classical economy is one in which the characteristic position is one of "dynamic equilibrium" in Champernowne's idiosyncratic sense that ongoing investment is taking place—not in the Harrodian sense of balanced growth. Champernowne's Classical case is depicted in Figure 5.1, where the equality between the demand and supply for savings is represented along the *IS* schedule and the equality between the demand and supply for money is represented along the *LM* schedule in interest rate and *money* wage (r, w) space while the equality between the demand and supply for labor is depicted in real wage and employment (W, N) space.[4]

In such a world, the economy self-adjusts to full employment via real-wage flexibility. There is no discrepancy between money wage bargains and the direction of change of the real wage. All real variables—employment and, implicitly, output—are determined by aggregate labor market clearing. Labor supply and labor demand depend solely on the real-wage rate. The interest rate and the nominal wage are determined

FIGURE 5.1

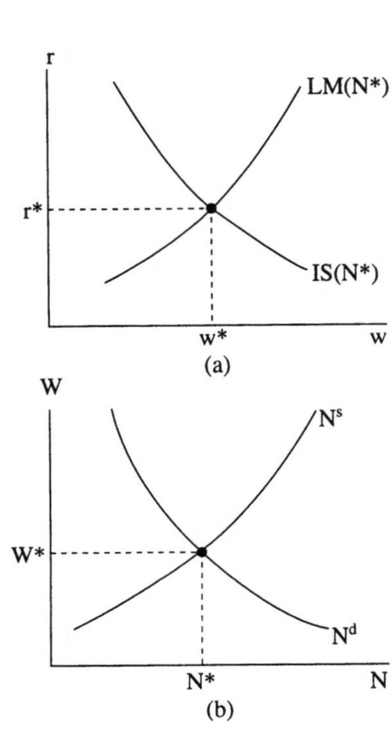

by the interaction of the markets for savings and for money. The unemployment rate corresponding to employment level N^* would be Champernowne's basic unemployment rate or Friedman's natural rate of unemployment.

The key modification of the model to produce Champernowne's version of the Keynesian system is the insertion of the money wage rate as a separate argument from the real wage in the labor supply equation. As Champernowne (1936, p. 212) put it, "in other words, Keynes takes account of monetary unemployment whereas the classical economists assume that all unemployment is basic." Labor, therefore, is concerned not only with its real wage but also with it money wage, and the elasticity of labor supply differs with respect to variations in each. In addition, Champernowne treats the supply of money as a function of the interest rate rather than being purely exogenous, and he introduces the variable Q into the savings demand (or investment) function and the variable Q' into the money demand function. Q and Q' are described as "certain influences such as general nervousness, the state of the news and effects due to the expectation of changes in the price-level, etc." (Champernowne, 1936, p. 211).

FIGURE 5.2

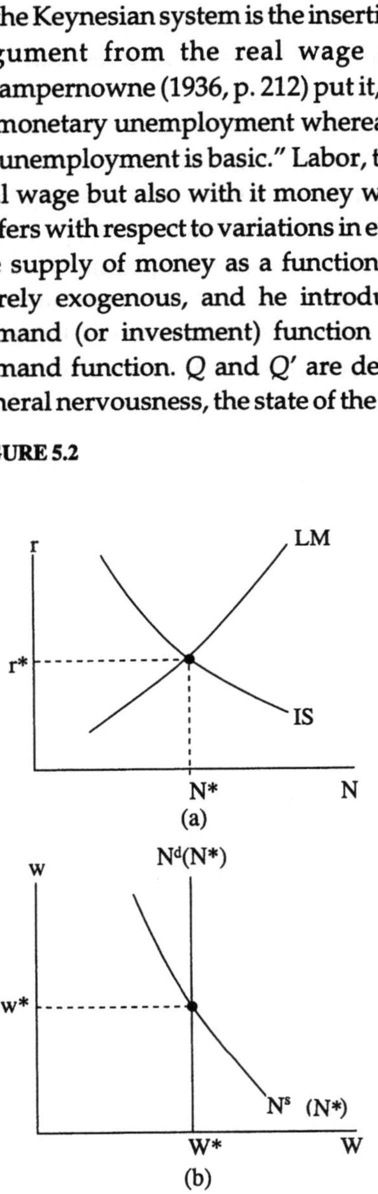

Since he treats Q and Q' as given during the short period—perhaps because the state of long-term expectation is treated as given—the presence of Q and Q' do not affect the analysis. It really is the inclusion of w in the labor supply function that transforms the story altogether from the classical story.

Champernowne's Keynesian system appears in Figure 5.2. Now the level of employment is not determined in the labor market. Indeed, there is no readily identifiable benchmark for full employment there. The employment level is determined by the intersection of the *IS* and *LM* schedules, and their position depends in turn on the conditions of aggregate demand, the volume of investment activity, and the size of the money stock. The unusual labor market determines the real price of labor and the nominal price of labor, taking the employment level as given. In a strict sense, Figure 5.2b does not represent a labor market at all, since the level of employment is predetermined. The N^s schedule in Figure 5.2b represents all combinations of money wage rates and real wage rates consistent with employment level N^*. A change in aggregate demand conditions or in the quantity of money that alters the employment level would result in a shift of both the N^d and N^s schedules in W, w space.

Where is full employment? What is the level of employment that is associated with the natural or basic rate? Perhaps these questions are not as troublesome as they might appear at first blush. After all, it can be argued that the presence of the nominal wage in the labor supply function is due only to irrational money illusion or labor's short-period inability to anticipate changes in the cost of living. In the long period only the real wage, W, should be in the labor supply function and the system will simplify to the classical framework, where, conceptually, full employment and both the natural and basic rates of unemployment are unambiguously associated with clearing of the aggregate labor market. The homogeneity postulate invariably drives the money wage out of the labor supply function.

But our objective here is merely foreshadowing. The point we seek to extract from Champernowne's Keynesian model is more general. If *either* aggregate labor supply or demand are sensitive to any endogenous variable besides the real wage, any straightforward link between labor market clearing and the full employment position of the economy is rendered untenable. But that is precisely the link that is made to arrive at the companion concepts of natural or basic unemployment rates. Our problems are just beginning to become apparent.

We turn next to Joan Robinson's (1937) discussion in her *Essays in the Theory of Employment*. Throughout the volume she uses two definitions of full employment, which she treats as equivalent—although, strictly speaking, they need not be. The first is a condition in which "the demand for labour is exactly equal to the supply" (p. 14) or "the point of intersection of the supply curve and the demand curve [for labour]" (p. 171). The second is a condition "when no one employer can increase his staff without reducing the staff of some other employer" or "one entrepreneur can increase the amount of labour he employs only by reducing the amount employed by someone else" (p. 15).

In the chapter of her text entitled "Diagrammatic Illustrations," Robinson (1937, p. 171) provides pictures of four major cases of full employment represented by the first of her two definitions—in which full employment is given by the intersection of the supply and demand schedules for labor. Her pictures, reproduced in our Figure 5.3, are drawn in real-wage and employment space (*W*, *N*). Robinson takes the position that labor market clearing defines full employment, and she is steadfast in that stance. Therefore, in each of the four cases *N** represents the full employment level of employment, and the associated unemployment rate would be the full employment unemployment rate.

Figure 5.3a is the familiar case of an upward-sloping labor supply curve and a downward-sloping labor demand curve. Figures 5.3b and 5.3c feature an upward-sloping labor demand curve. The rationale seems to be an efficiency wage effect; labor productivity rises with each increase in real wages.[5] Figures 5.3c and 5.3d feature a downward-sloping labor supply

FIGURE 5.3

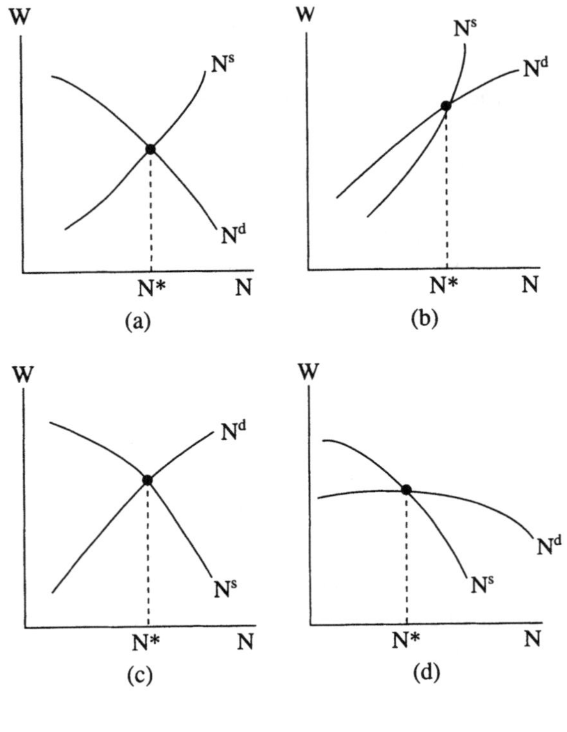

schedule, the backward-rising labor supply schedule often attributed to the mercantilist writers who antedated Adam Smith. Both of these unorthodox shapes are given justification in the following passage: "A rise in the level of real wages will have effects which tell in opposite directions. On the one hand it will raise the personal efficiency of the workers by improving their standard of life; on the other hand, as needs becomes less urgent, the choice between an increase in leisure and an increase in earnings is likely to turn more in favour of leisure, in spite of the extra inducement to work represented by a higher rate of reward." (Robinson, 1937, p. 164).

Robinson (1937, p. 167) also invokes an additional effect, which suggests that recent unemployment rates should enter both the labor demand and labor supply functions, laying the foundations for an unemployment hysterisis argument: "The level of unemployment experienced over a number of years will affect the supply curve of labour in other ways. On the one hand a high level of unemployment, just as much as a low level of real wages, may lead to a loss of efficiency and so cause the available supply of labour to fall off. On the other hand, hours and intensity of work are increased not only by a fall in real wages but also by an increase in insecurity, which causes workers to placate their employers, in fear of losing their jobs by working hard and refraining from complaints about unpleasant conditions."[6]

Elsewhere, we (Goldsmith and Darity, 1992) have described these two conflicting effects on labor supply as the discouragement and trauma-escape effects. Which of the two is dominant will determine the direction of shift in the labor-supply schedule in response to increased exposure of the labor force to unemployment. But the loss in productivity also should lower the demand for labor, while the trauma-escape effect, if it results in more disciplined workers, should raise the demand for labor. And, again, which effect is dominant will dictate the shift in the labor demand schedule induced by exposure to unemployment.

This line of argument implies a feedback effect from current and recent employment and unemployment onto the current level of employment. Indeed, Robinson (1937, pp. 167–68) observes, immediately after this discussion, "such considerations show one of the imperfections of the method of treating the available supply of labour in a given population as a function of real wages alone." Her own work epitomizes the confusion that is created by recognizing that the real wage is not the sole argument of the labor supply (or demand) functions while simultaneously using the intersection of supply and demand schedules to define full employment.

Consider the situation depicted in Figure 5.4. We have conventionally sloped labor supply and demand schedules drawn in real wage and employment (*W*, *N*) space. We assume that the recent history of unemployment will shift the schedules, and we will assume that the trauma-escape effect dominates the discouragement effect. The economy starts at position *A* with real wage W^* and employment level N^*, where the labor market clears. Now assume, in the current vernacular, that a shock occurs—such as an overnight loss of a portion of the capital stock—that causes the labor demand schedule to shift to the left from *Nd* to *Nd'*. Employment falls from N^* to *N*; real wages fall from W^* to *W'*; and the labor force is exposed to a higher rate of unemployment along the path from *A* to *B*.

FIGURE 5.4

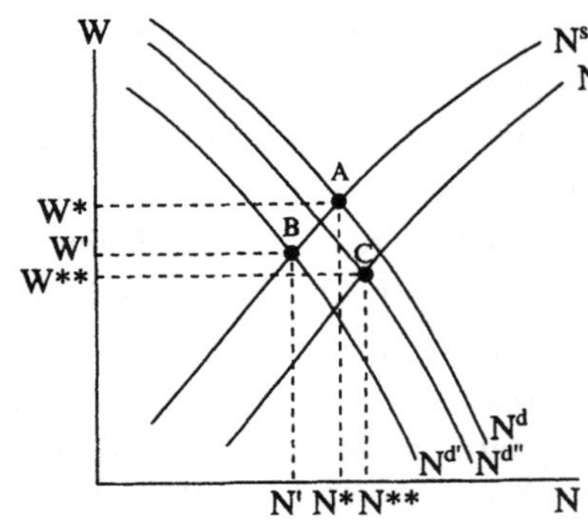

But if the trauma-escape effect dominates the discouragement effect, desperate workers should be willing to offer more hours at any real wage. The labor-supply schedule should shift to the right in response to the increased exposure to unemployment. Employers, recognizing that workers's insecurities will lead them to be more productive, also may increase their demand for labor, and, therefore, the labor-demand schedule will shift to the right. The economy could then move toward a position like C, with employment level N^{**}. Note that N', N^*, and N^{**} are all positions in which the labor market clears labor supply and labor demand are equal at all three positions. But which one is full employment? Do we call all three full employment?

To further complicate matters note the inconsistency that arises between Joan Robinson's two central definitions of full employment. At positions *A* and *C* labor supply and demand are equal. But if the economy moves from *A* to *C*, an employer hiring a new worker need not be taking that person from another employer since the total employment is higher at position C than at *A*.

Now, it may be easy to counter this type of argument at the empirical level, to claim that the social psychological effects are slow, that these shifts do not occur rapidly enough in real time to matter. Therefore, N^* may constrain the total amount of labor available to employers when the aggregate labor market clears.

But at the theoretical level both Champernowne's and Robinson's analyses indicate that the labor market clearing notion of full employment is insufficient. In Champernowne's Keynesian framework the presence of the money wage in the labor supply obliterates the possibility of identifying the full employment position in the labor market altogether. In Joan Robinson's analysis, if unemployment rates enter the labor demand and supply functions, we would be compelled to call a wide range of employment levels "full employment," if we stayed wedded to Robinson's own first definition of full employment.

Furthermore, there are other possible shift variables that could enter into the labor-demand and labor-supply functions that could operate more quickly than unemployment exposure. Consider Don Patinkin's awareness in the 1950s of the limitations associated with saying that full employment is defined by labor-market clearing. In his development of microfoundations for aggregate functions, Patinkin displayed an unbending commitment to consistency—until he gets to the labor market. His labor market looks remarkably like Champernowne's version of the classical labor market, with labor supply and demand functions that depend exclusively on the real wage. Patinkin's (1956, p. 129) candor with respect to his choice of specification bears restatement here: "It will immediately be recognized that we have greatly oversimplified the analysis of this market [the labor market]. Both the demand and supply functions for labor should actually be presented as dependent on the real value of bond and money holdings as well as the real wage rate. Furthermore, if we were to permit the firm to vary its input of capital, its demand for labor would also depend on the rate of interest. Finally, a full utility analysis of individual behavior would show the supply of labor also to depend on this rate."

If the labor-supply function and -demand functions were specified as follows—$N_s = N_s(W, r, B/P, M/P)$ and $N_d = N_d(W, r, B/P, M/P)$—monetary policy could have a direct effect on the labor market. There would be more than one position where $N_s = N_d$ as r, M, B or P vary. Which of these positions are full employment? Patinkin seemed to say, who knows? Therefore, it would be simpler to bypass these other effects on aggregate labor supply and demand altogether to remove all ambiguity from market clearing and full employment: "If we have cavalierly ignored these additional influences, it is because the labor market as such does not interest us in the following analysis; its sole function is to provide the benchmark of full employment"

(Patinkin, 1956, p. 129). With fully specified labor-supply and -demand schedules, the benchmark of full employment would have been lost. And so Don Patinkin (1956, pp. 212–213) went down the road to disequilibrium macroeconomics, as the true forerunner of New Keynesian economics, with workers being involuntarily unemployed if they were "off their supply curve."

In addition to the nominal wage, the recent history of unemployment rates, the rate of interest, real bond holdings, and real cash balances, there are other candidates for shift effects that permeate the literature. Wealth effects generally can matter; Ghez and Becker (1975) have argued that additional wealth reduces the supply of labor. Expectations of layoffs can lead to alterations in labor supply and real wages as well (see Hamermesh and Wolf, 1990; Topel, 1984; Filer, 1986; and Li, 1986). Changes in the probability of promotion will affect labor supply in a fashion analogous to changes in the probability of being laid off (Hall, 1988). There are also potential aggregate productivity effects of human capital accumulation (Goldsmith, 1983; Romer, 1990). Charles Holt (1980) has argued that not only should the unemployment rate enter into labor-demand and -supply functions but also the vacancy rate.

Given the foregoing, it is striking that Keynes never adopted a concept of full employment tied to labor-market clearing in either *The General Theory* or thereafter. Full employment was not determined in the labor market or by labor-market clearing for Keynes (see Darity and Horn, 1983).

The first definition of involuntary unemployment Keynes (1936, p. 15, emphasis in original) offers in *The General Theory* is the following: "Men are involuntarily unemployed if, in the event of a small rise in the price of wage-goods relative to the money-wage, both the aggregate supply of labour willing to work for the current money-wage and the aggregate demand for it at that wage would be greater than the existing volume of employment." Understandably, this definition could appear to be a convoluted procedure for saying full employment is defined by the intersection of labor demand and supply functions, *à la* Joan Robinson in 1937.

Consider Robinson's first case in her Figure 3 (case 3a). If the real wage is above the market-clearing position in a one-sector economy where both labor demand and supply functions depend on nothing but the real-wage rate, we can ask what happens if there is a "small rise in the price of wage-goods relative to the money-wage."

We reproduce this case with more detail in Figure 5.5, where, at the original disequilibrium real wage W'', the level of employment is N'' and there is an excess supply of labor, since workers want to offer *N*2 units of labor. If the small rise in the price of wage goods occurs, presumably the real wage will decline. Employers will move down their labor-demand schedule to hire more labor—say, *N′* hours of labor. Workers also will move down their labor-supply schedule and reduce the hours of labor they offer to *N*1, but both *N′* and *N*1 are larger than the original level of employment *N″*. So by Keynes's definition, involuntary unemployment existed when *N″* hours of labor were hired. And there will be involuntary unemployment in this sense until the real wage falls to *W** and *N** units of labor are hired. On the face of it, Keynes has said nothing more than that involuntary unemployment exists when labor supply is greater than labor demand. But now examine Joan Robinson's case 3d in which there is a standard labor-demand schedule but a downward-sloping labor-supply schedule. Suppose the initial position is the one in which the labor market clears with real wage *W** and employment level *N**, and suppose that the real wage falls due, again, to a small rise in the price of wage goods. Now excess demand will have been imposed in the labor market. Employers will want to hire more labor than *N**, and workers will want to supply more labor than *N**. Although the labor market cleared at *N**, involuntary unemployment existed on the basis of Keynes's definition.

FIGURE 5.5

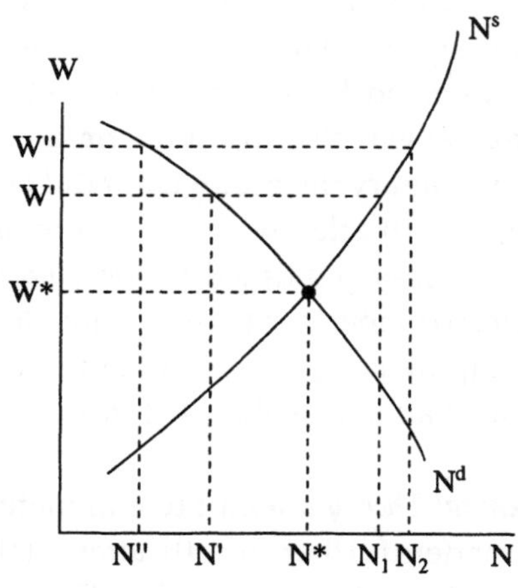

Joan Robinson (1937, p. 172, n. 1) was struck by this seeming anomaly and observed, "[Mr. Keynes's] condition [for involuntary unemployment] is fulfilled by the level of employment [N*] in [my] Fig. 7 at which there is no involuntary unemployment." But, of course, by Keynes's definition there was involuntary unemployment at *N**. There was none for Joan Robinson, who was captivated, unlike Keynes, by the ready-made identification of full employment with the market clearing position.

At the core of Keynes's definition is a policy activist's experiment. How do you bring about a rise in the price of wage goods? You expand aggregate demand and ask whether both labor supply and demand are higher compared with the previous level of employment. Keynes's first definition in *The General Theory* requires a fall in the real-wage rate, perhaps attributable to Keynes's belief at the time that real movements were countercyclical. But his subsequent definitions preserved the policy experiment without the requirement that real wages fall.

For example, in *The General Theory* Keynes gives his second definition, which he treats as identical to the first: "An alternative, though equivalent criterion [for full employment] is that at which we have now arrived, namely a situation in which aggregate employment is inelastic in response to an increase in the effective demand for its output." [p. 26]. The definition is not "equivalent." It sets no constraints on the movement of real wages; it says simply that the economy is at full employment when there is no additional employment bang for the aggregate demand buck. And it is irrelevant whether or not the aggregate labor market was clearing at the time.

The multiplicity of definitions of involuntary unemployment did create some confusion, which Keynes (1973, p. 110) acknowledged shortly after publication of *The General Theory* in an essay published in the *Quarterly Journal of Economics*: "In regard to Professor Viner's criticisms of my definition and treatment of involuntary unemployment, I am ready to agree that this part of my book is open to criticism. I already feel myself in a position to make improvements."

Unfortunately, in an early post-*General Theory* attempt to eliminate the confusion, Keynes actually muddled matters further. Shortly after publication Keynes (1973, p. 71) wrote in a letter dated August 31, 1936,[7] "I have not dealt perhaps as fully as I should with the relation between involuntary unemployment and transfer difficulties. I regard transfer difficulties as reducing a man's efficiency for the available employment. But I regard his employment as involuntary as long as the reward he could earn after allowing for this reduction in efficiency remains greater than his minimum terms." In short, Keynes is arguing that if workers are displaced from a particular line of industry, the search unemployment they incur is involuntary, even if the market clearing wage in the new sector where the worker eventually finds employment exceeds his or her proper minimum.

Search unemployment induced by displacements or layoffs are not the responsibility nor fault of labor. If sectoral shifts are at the base of search unemployment, Keynes counts that unemployment as involuntary in nature. Thus, he offers still another definition of involuntary unemployment.

Only those searching who are new entrants, reentrants, or job quitters seeking employment in the same sector could qualify as voluntarily unemployed.

The letter, sent from Keynes to Hicks, did not elucidate matters further, and Hicks, unsurprisingly, was not satisfied. Indeed, it appears that he proceeded to press Keynes to reveal whether one must meet *all* or just any of the criteria for unemployment to be designated involuntary. In a letter to Keynes dated September 2, 1936, Hicks inquired (Keynes, 1973, p. 73): "I do not want to give up my substantial point, that output may have reached a short-period maximum, even when there are a considerable number of unemployed specialized to the investment goods industries. But I take it you would accept this and redefine full employment to cover this case."

To understand Hicks's query, note that by Keynes's third definition of involuntary unemployment, those persons frictionally unemployed due to job displacement count among the involuntarily unemployed. However, aggregate employment may be unchanged and may be insensitive to aggregate demand expansion. On the basis of the second definition of involuntary unemployment, the economy is at full employment or void of involuntary unemployment.

Hicks is asking Keynes if the outcome of his policy experiment to test for involuntary unemployment dominates the presence of other sources of involuntary unemployment. Specifically, if aggregate demand expansion fails to alter employment, even if some other criterion for involuntary unemployment is met, is the economy at full employment? Hicks expects Keynes to answer in the affirmative.

Keynes (1973, pp. 74–75) appears to have misinterpreted or reinterpreted Hicks's point; he replied to Hicks in a letter dated September 8, 1936: "I agree with your point that output may have reached a short-period maximum even when there are a considerable number of unemployed specialized in skill or locality, who are not worth their minimum terms in the employment which an increase in effective demand would make available. I ought to have emphasized and explained this, but it does not, I think, require a formally new definition of full employment. The definition I gave in my previous letter is formally equivalent, I think, with that which I gave in my book." By circling us back to *The General Theory* for clarification, Keynes left unanswered the original puzzle Hicks submitted. If there is search unemployment due to displacement, which Keynes designates as involuntary unemployment in his correspondence with Hicks, accompanied by a situation in which a demand expansion fails to alter employment, which Keynes designates as a condition of full employment in *The General Theory*, is the economy at full employment or not? At that early stage the issue remained muddled.

Although Keynes said that he believed that he had addressed adequately the issue of a hierarchical status of alternative definitions of involuntary unemployment, he was unwilling to be explicit with Hicks. However, after reading a draft of Roy Harrod's article "Mr. Keynes and Traditional Theory," Keynes (1973, pp. 85–86) wrote Harrod on August 30, 1936: "You do not show how in conditions of full employment, which I should now like to define as the limiting case in which the supply of output schedule ceases to be elastic, my theory merges in the orthodox theory." Based on Keynes's response to Harrod, it can be inferred that a hierarchy exists and that the policy experiment sits atop. Moreover, it is evident that Keynes gave much thought to the *concept* of full employment after the appearance of *The General Theory*. For instance, in Keynes's (1973, pp. 104–106) contribution to the Fisher *festschrift* the following quotations appear: "The scale of investment will not reach its equilibrium until the point is reached at which the elasticity of supply of output as a whole has fallen to zero. A zero elasticity of supply for output as a whole means that an increase of demand in terms of money will lead to no change in output; that is to say, prices will rise in the same proportion as the money demand rises. Inflation will have no effect on output or employment, but only on prices . . . a zero elasticity of supply for output involves a zero elasticity of supply for employment; there is in my terminology full employment. Indeed, the condition in which the elasticity of the supply of output as a [whole is zero, is, I now think, the most convenient criterion for defining full employment." Now a different distinction can be drawn between Keynes's view of involuntary unemployment and that of the classicals, from that drawn by Champernowne. For the classicals, if involuntary unemployment was to have any meaning, it had to involve the prevalence of nonmarket clearing wages; for Keynes, in contrast, involuntary unemployment meant that the economy had come to rest at a level of employment lower than would prevail if a boost was given to aggregate demand.

It is hard to say whether Champernowne's or Joan Robinson's efforts to conceptualize involuntary unemployment on ostensibly Keynesian terms mattered to Keynes or influenced Keynes. No extant documents indicate Keynes's reaction to Champernowne's article. Keynes's (1973, pp. 134–48) correspondence with Joan Robinson over her essays was lukewarm at best and certainly not enthusiastic. Joan Robinson's influence certainly is not apparent in the definitions Keynes adopted in his post-*General Theory* writings and correspondence.

Keynes ultimately arrived at a criterion for full employment independent of the aggregate labor market. Basic versus monetary unemployment, money illusion, efficiency wages, unemployment exposure and macroeconomics all were part and parcel of Cambridge employment analysis in the late 1930s. These were materials with which Keynes was quite familiar, but he did not embrace them nor tailor his definition of full employment to conform to them. His definitions were not based on labor market disequilibrium; his approach was not that of the New Keynesians. Even in *The General Theory* Keynes suggests that the labor market-clearing notion of full employment is inadequate. In the appendix to Chapter 19 where he excoriates Pigou, his attack centers on the incomplete specification of the labor demand and supply equations he attributes to Pigou. In particular, in the context of Pigou's two-sector framework Keynes argues that Pigou's inattention to sectoral interactions and sectoral differences in employment elasticities leads to an unsound analysis of the determinants of employment and the full employment level.

The New Keynesians use Joan Robinson's criterion for full employment —supply of labor equals demand for labor. To treat involuntary unemployment they are driven to invoke price and wage rigidities. Taking such rigidities as a datum, they then seek to explain the rigidities as the outcome of maximizing behavior by economic agents, which they explain via informational asymmetries, efficiency wages, and monopolistic competition.

All of this has nothing to do with Keynes, whose very concept of involuntary unemployment was not linked to price inflexibility. Again, note the extended examination in Chapter 19 of *The General Theory* of the effects of money-wage flexibility and the incapacity of such flexibility to ensure arrival at full employment. To the extent that one pursues Keynes's conceptualization of involuntary unemployment, the New Keynesian research agenda becomes unnecessary, and the natural rate of unemployment becomes an empty concept. After all, if the natural rate of unemployment is any rate of unemployment associated with labor-market clearing, but labor-market clearing lacks the connotation of full employment, then there is nothing special about the natural rate of unemployment. Keynes's conceptualization of involuntary unemployment, independent of the labor market, disconnects the notion of full employment from equality of supply and demand in a putative aggregate labor market.

The New Keynesians, while investing vast time and effort in explaining why labor markets do not clear, actually sanctify the intersection of labor supply and demand schedules. They then spend all their time trying to establish why such an intersection is not attained. This is, if anything, as Michael Lawlor (1991) has suggested a "New Pigovian" research agenda. Indeed, in Robert Solow's (1980, pp. 3–4) presidential address to the American Economic Association in which he cataloged the various lines of approach to labor market disequilibrium subsequently pursued by the New Keynesian, it was Pigou's works rather than Keynes's that were given pride of place. We contend that a genuinely Keynesian research agenda would focus not on the variegated foibles of the aggregate labor market but on the theory of investment and the rehabilitation of the multiplier. In particular, the Keynesian researcher's deepest concern would be with the effects of expectations and uncertainty and financial and monetary policy on investment. What makes investment activity accelerate? What makes it slow down? What accounts for its volatility? How do business people's perceptions and psychological bent affect fixed capital formation? This, of course, is far from an alien research agenda for economists; this is the passion of Tobin and Brainard (1977) among many others. But it is the research agenda that flows naturally from Keynes's inquiry.

But to make graphic the limitations of the New Keynesian approach, consider the hypothetical situation depicted in Figure 5.6. Suppose the initial position of the economy is at point *A* with real wage *W′* and employment level *N′*. Suppose, further, that a significant portion of the nation's capital stock is destroyed, leading to a collapse in the demand for labor. At the new equilibrium at point B, the real wage has fallen to *W″* and employment to *N″*. At both points *A* and *B* the labor market clears, but at widely discrepant levels of activity. Should both levels of employment be viewed as full employment? For the New Keynesians both must be; for Keynes point B definitely is not because government expenditure to promote

FIGURE 5.6

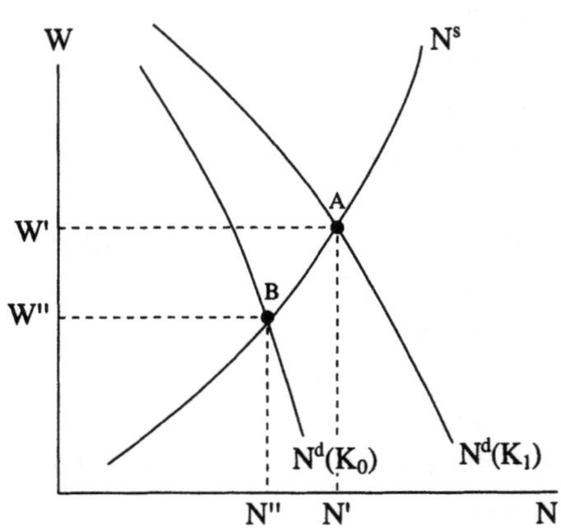

investment activity will cause the labor demand schedule to shift rightward, raising employment. Both *A* and *B* are Walrasian equilibria, but certainly *B* does not have the dint of optimality about it.

Keynes (1936, p. 183) expressed skepticism about the usefulness of the concept of the natural rate of interest, since any natural rate would be an equilibrium rate but not the rate of interest associated with full employment. He preferred instead the idea of the *neutral* rate of interest: "I am now no longer of the opinion that the concept of a "natural" rate of interest, which previously seemed to me a most promising idea, has anything very useful or significant to contribute to our analysis. It is merely the rate of interest which will preserve the *status quo*; and, in general, we have no predominant interest in the *status quo* as such. If there is any such rate of interest, which is unique and significant, it must be the rate which we might term the *neutral* rate of interest, namely the natural rate . . . which is consistent with full employment, given the other parameters of the system" (emphasis in original).

In parallel fashion the concept of the natural rate of unemployment is not particularly useful either (also see Isaac). Rather, we propose that the more valuable concept is the *neutral* rate of unemployment—the rate of unemployment that prevails when there is no further payoff in terms of employment if an aggregate demand expansion takes place. Because there is a multiplicity of potential positions—the labor market clears—there are many, many natural rates of unemployment, but "given the other parameters of the system," there is only one neutral rate associated with the absence of Keynes's involuntary unemployment. It is at the neutral rate of unemployment that the classical (or new classical, for that matter) economics comes back into play, but the fact that the labor market clears, in and of itself, does not put the economy in a classical (or new classical) environment.

NOTES

1. Note that Champernowne's use of the concepts of short and long periods appear to be in calendar time and is quite distinct from Keynes's (1936) own usage of the concepts in Chapter 5 of *The General Theory*.

2. The potential brake on deflation set by the real balance or Pigou effect is not present in Champernowne's argument, perhaps simply because Pigou had yet to advance this possibility. Regardless, in principle, the Pigou effect can be offset or dominated by the Fisher effect, the negative consequences for aggregate demand of the deteriorating net worth positions of debtors in the face of price declines (Tobin, 1980, pp.9–12).

3. Although it should be mentioned that Champernowne (1936, p. 204, n. 1) also is the author of the following inscrutable footnote: "The concept of Monetary Unemployment is copied from Keynes's Involuntary Unemployment . . . but differs from that concept."

4. Champernowne suppresses real income in his analysis, treating all functions in which real income is an argument as directly dependent on the level of employment instead. So, for example, in Champernowne's Keynesian model savings depends on the level of employment rather than real income.

5. The New Keynesians use the efficiency wage argument to provide a rational basis for wage stickiness (see, e.g. Summers, 1988, and Yellen, 1988), while Robinson incorporated this effect directly into the shape of the labor demand function under market clearing circumstances.

6. Robinson (1937, p. 167, n. 1) says in a footnote, "The weakening of resistance may take the form of willingness to work longer hours for the same daily wage. The paradoxical expedient of lengthening the working day in the face of severe unemployment is not unknown in practice."

7. The letter was prompted by John Hicks's (1936) review of *The General Theory* in the *Economic Journal*.

REFERENCES

Adams, C., and D. T. Coe. (1990). "A Systems Approach to Estimating the Natural Rate of Unemployment and Potential Output for the United States." *IMF Staff Papers*, 37, 232–293.

Cain, Glen C. (1979). "The Unemployment Rate as an Economic Indicator." *Monthly Labor Review*, March, 25–34.

Champernowne, David G. (1936). "Unemployment, Basic and Monetary: The Classical Analysis and the Keynesian." *Review of Economic Studies*, 3, 201–216.

Darity, William A., Jr., and Bobbie L. Horn. (1983). "Involuntary Unemployment Reconsidered." *Southern Economic Journal*, 49, 717–733.

Feldstein, Martin. (1973). *Lowering the Permanent Rate of Unemployment*. Washington, D.C.: U.S. Government Printing Office.

Filer, Randall K. (1986). "The Effect of Nonpecuniary Compensation on Estimates of Labor Supply Functions." *Quarterly Review of Economics and Business*, 26, 17–30.

Friedman, Milton. (1968). "The Role of Monetary Policy." *American Economic Review*, (March), 1–17.

Ghez, G. R., and G. S. Becker. (1975). *The Allocation of Time and Goods Over the Life Cycle*. New York: Columbia University Press.

Goldsmith, Arthur. (1983). "Short-Run Macroeconomic Consequences of Government Financial Human Capital Expenditures." *Quarterly Review of Economics and Business*, 23, 89–107.

Goldsmith, Arthur, and William Darity, Jr. (1992). "Social Psychology, Unemployment Exposure and Equilibrium Unemployment." *Journal of Economic Psychology*, 13 (3), 449–471.

Hall, Robert E. (1988). "Fluctuations in Equilibrium Unemployment." *American Economic Review*, 78, 269–275.

Hamermesh, Daniel S., and John R. Wolfe. (1990). "Compensating Wage Differentials and the Duration of Wage Loss." *Journal of Labor Economics*, 8 (1, p. 2), 175–197.

Hicks, J. R. (1936). "Mr. Keynes's Theory of Employment." *The Economic Journal*, 46, 238–253.

Holt, Charles. (1980). "Wages and Job Availability in Segmented Labor Markets." In Edmond Malinvaud and Jean-Paul Fitoussi (Eds.), *Unemployment in Western Countries*, 385–408. New

York: St. Martin's Press.

Isaac, Alan G. (1991). "Is There a Natural Rate?" Working paper, Department of Economics, American University.

Keynes, J. M. (1936). *The General Theory of Employment, Interest and Money*. London: Macmillan.

———. (1973). *Collected Writings of John Maynard Keynes*, Vol. 14, edited by Donald Moggridge. London: Macmillan.

Lawlor, M. S. (1991). "Keynes, Cambridge and the New Keynesian Economics." In W. Darity, Jr. (Ed.). *Controversies in Labor Economics*. Boston: Kluwer.

Li, Elizabeth H. (1986). "Compensating Differentials for Cyclical and Noncyclical Unemployment: The Interaction between Investors's and Employees's Risk Aversion." *Journal of Labor Economics*, 4, 277–296.

Patinkin, Don. (1956). *Money, Interest and Prices: An Integration of Monetary and Value Theory*. Evanston, IL: Row, Peterson.

Robinson, Joan. (1937). *Essays in the Theory of Employment*. London: Macmillan.

Romer, Paul. (1990). "Endogenous Technological Change." *Journal of Political Economy*, 98 (5, p2) 71–102.

Salemi, Michael K. (1991). "A Dynamic Factor Model Approach to Estimating the Natural Rate of Unemployment and the Phillips Curve." Working paper, University of North Carolina at Chapel Hill (July).

Salop, Steven. (1979). "A Model of the Natural Rate of Unemployment." *American Economic Review*, 69, 117–125.

Solow, Robert M. (1980). "On Theories of Unemployment." *American Economic Review* (March), 1–11.

Summers, Lawrence. (1986). "Why Is the Unemployment Rate So Very High near Full Employment?" *Brookings Papers on Economic Activity*, 2, 339–383.

———. (1988). "Relative Wages, Efficiency Wages and Keynesian Unemployment." *American Economic Review*, 78, 383–388.

Tobin, James, and William Brainard. (1977). "Asset Market and the Cost of Capital." *Economic Progress, Private Values and Public Policy: Essays in Honor of William Fellner*, pp. 235–262. Amsterdam: North-Holland.

———. (1980). *Asset Accumulation and Economic Activity*. Chicago: University of Chicago Press.

Topel, R. H. (1984). "Equilibrium Earnings, Turnover, and Unemployment: New Evidence." *Journal of Labor Economics*, 2, 500–522.

Yellen, Janet L. (1984). "Efficiency Wage Models of Unemployment." *American Economic Review*, 74, 200–205.

Young, Warren. (1987). *Interpreting Mr. Keynes: The IS-LM Enigma*. London: Basil Blackwell.

6

Causes for Persistent Unemployment and Fluctuations in Monetary Economies

Edward J. Amadeo

6.1

Capitalist economies follow different patterns of fluctuation. If we think of the rate of unemployment as a measure of the movements of the economy, we note that the patterns of fluctuation vary across time and across countries. After World War II, unemployment remained very low in all advanced capitalist economies up until the late 1960s, then started fluctuating around a much higher rate in the 1970s and 1980s. In certain European countries, the average rate of unemployment in the 1980s was significantly higher than the OECD average and much higher than what it was in the 1950s and 1960s.

What accounts for the differences in patterns of fluctuations and in averages around which economies fluctuate? There is no complete answer to this question, and the answer to it cannot be the object of this article. However, I do try to discuss issues associated with this general question. In particular, based on Keynes's views on the properties of monetary economies, the article is intended to highlight the factors accounting for economic fluctuations.

The second section discusses the operation of barter economies to show that, in principle, the existence of time and money is not required to impede the possibility of isolated bargains and decisions determining real variables. Section 6.3 explores the properties of money that led Keynes to emphasize the differences between barter and monetary economies. Section 6.4 examines Keynes's criticism of the classical theory. In section 6.5 the notion of involuntary unemployment is presented based on *The General Theory*'s static equilibrium position. The factors accounting for fluctuations in monetary economies are discussed in section 6.6. Section 6.7 looks at Keynes's view on the causes of persistent unemployment. Section 6.8 concludes by arguing that current orthodox macroeconomic thought dismisses Keynes's view on the ineffective workings of market economies based on dogmatic grounds.

6.2. Nominal Decisions and Real Outcomes

In a barter economy, people exchange goods for goods or for promises to receive goods in the future. In particular, workers exchange human effort for goods. Let us take this wonderland one step further and assume that only one good exists. In such case, workers would work only enough to receive the amount of the good they want to consume and save. In this very special world, workers and firms would negotiate over the *real* wage (units of the good per hour of work) and firms would be certain about the amount to produce. As noted by Chick (1983, p. 294): "If workers are paid in kind, it is conceivable that they receive directly, as payment, the goods they wish to consume. In that circumstance, not only do employers know the demand implications of the labour they hire, but labour also knows the consumption potential of an hour's work, i.e. labour is demanded and supplied for a real wage which is *known* to both parties."

The situation is different if there is more than one good. For then, if workers were paid in kind, they would have to trade the goods in which they are paid for the goods they want to consume. In this situation, a vector of market prices would arise from the interaction of supply and demand for the goods at each period. Assume that firms produce only to pay their respective workers. Firms would still be sure of selling their output, but workers would not be sure about the purchasing power of their wage the relative value of the basket of goods they receive at the end of the period. However, if the firm pays its workers in kind and sells the surplus in the market, it will not be sure of the price for which the goods will be sold. Hence, in this circumstances, firms would also face uncertainty.

The multigoods system invites the appearance of monies: indeed, money first appeared to facilitate trade. A monetary economy is primarily one in which goods are traded for money. Labor is traded for money, and like all other prices, the *money* wage is denominated in money terms. Firms pay workers in money and sell goods for money. Firms buy machines for money and sell the goods produced with the machine for money. Because relative prices and the price of money in terms of goods change over time, in monetary multigoods economies agents exchange goods for money and do not know exactly the purchasing power of their receipts.

However, as long as money performs only the role of means of exchange, its existence is immaterial for the phenomenon discussed here. Indeed, for the possibility of windfall gains or losses of workers, producers and investors, it does not really matter which good or goods are used as means of payment. In barter economies with many goods, contracts are denominated in terms of a numeraire that has a variable value in terms of the other goods. The *real* price (in terms of any numeraire) of a good depends on the movement of relative prices. The later depend on the interaction of decisions of decentralized agents, and the individual agent cannot know for certain what the outcome of this interaction will be.

We usually think of time as an essential element in generating discrepancies between nominal and real prices or between expected and actual prices. Indeed, time is important to the extent that most contracts and decisions refer to future payments, and current prices do not provide a good signal of prospective prices. However, what is really crucial is the uncertainty associated with the decentralization of decisions that is, the fact that agents negotiate and make decisions without really knowing what other parties are deciding. The compilation of a set of *spot* trades in an economy with many agents and many goods would certainly lead to windfall gains to some and losses to other agents. In principle, time does not have to elapse to create unexpected outcomes. Time surely adds uncertainty. Things that are taken for given in timeless cases may change as time elapses.

In sum, in an economy with many goods, in which atomized and uncoordinated decisions and transactions based on expectations are the rule, agents cannot be thought to trade over real variables. All transactions are denominated in money terms, and the real outcomes will depend on the interaction of a multitude of decisions and bargains in the economy. It is interesting to note that this result does not depend on the existence of money or time.

3.3. The Essential Role of Money

Again, the possibility of windfall gains or losses of agents in a market economy does not depend in any essential way on the existence of money as a means of exchange or time. The importance of money in Keynes's thought is associated with fact that money as a store of value is a good in itself in a system in which time elapses. As a means of exchange, money facilitates life, but no one would hoard money beyond a certain amount only because it minimizes transaction costs. The decision to hold money for transaction motives is rather mechanical, and the ratio of transaction demand to income is very stable.

However, agents do hold money and quasi-monies beyond the point determined by the transaction requirements. They do so because the possession of money provides them with a reward namely, liquidity or marketability. Agents keep assets for their prospective return (interests on bonds or equities or profits resulting from the use of capital goods), and they keep money for its liquidity.

The benefits of possessing money a barren but liquid asset varies over time. The preference for liquidity increases when, in face of a changing or unstable environment, agents find it difficult to form expectations over the prospective yield of assets and, therefore, do not want to commit themselves with assets of doubtful marketability. The result of an increase in liquidity preference is a rise in the rate of interest, which Keynes thought of as a premium for giving up liquidity. An increase in the rate of interest has a host of effects on the decisions taken by economic agents. In particular, it tends to reduce the propensity to consume and the incentives to invest. In a recession it would be desirable to have a decline in the rate of interest in order to activate aggregate demand.

It is the role of money as a store of value and the liquidity premium attached to it that Keynes probably had in mind when in 1933 he wrote that "the theory which I desiderate would deal . . . with an economy in which money plays a part of its own and affects motives and decisions" (Keynes, XIII, p. 408). Keynes referred to this theory as *the monetary theory of production.*

6.4. Keynes's Criticism of the Classical Theory

Keynes criticized the orthodoxy of his time on many grounds.[1] It is very difficult to provide a cohesive view of the critiques, but an attempt can be made. To concentrate on essentials and to maintain the objectivity of the argument, two objections to the classical theory seem crucial.

First, Keynes criticized the orthodox economists for maintaining that "the wage bargains between the entrepreneurs and the workers determine the real wage . . . so that [the workers] can, if they wish, bring their real wages into conformity with the marginal disutility of the amount of employment offered by the employers at that wage" (Keynes, VII, p. 11). The bargain over real wages presupposes that the levels of employment and output are determined in the labor market and correspond to the level of full employment of labor.

Keynes argued that workers negotiate money (not real) wages with entrepreneurs based on their expectations of the price level. Given the wage, firms fix the amount of employment based on the expected price of their product. The actual real wage of workers and product wage of the firm will depend on the evolution of the consumer price index and the market price of the good produced, respectively. Both depend on the interactions between the decisions made in other spheres of the economy. The first objection is thus related to the notion discussed in Section 6.2 that in market economies, agents cannot negotiate over real variables, only money variables.

An important contribution of *The General Theory* was the systematic analysis of the determinants of aggregate demand. Keynes's point was that the level of aggregate demand could be insufficient to absorb the output produced, in which case producers would revise their expectations and reduce the level of employment at the going wage.

Second, Keynes also criticizes the orthodoxy for "rest[ing] the supposedly self-adjusting character of the economic system on an assumed fluidity of money-wages; and, when there is rigidity, to lay on this rigidity the blame of maladjustment" (Keynes, VII, p. 257). In the *Treatise on Money* Keynes saw in money-wage rigidity the main cause of prolonged unemployment. A reduction in money wages and prices would increase the level of real balances and reduce the real wage thus closing the gap between investment and the level of full-employment saving. The *Treatise* was thus part of the orthodoxy that Keynes criticized in *The General Theory*. In the latter book, as I shall note in the following section, Keynes did not see the flexibility of money wages as a remedy to unemployment.

The treatment of changes in money wages is pivotal in Keynes's criticism of orthodox thinking in macroeconomics, for it dismisses any logically unambiguous movement of the economy toward full employment.

6.5. Equilibrium and Involuntary Unemployment

By noting that agents cannot negotiate over real variables, not even in barter economies, we eliminate the possibility of real wages and employment being determined in the labor market. This is the essential message of Keynes's first criticism to orthodoxy. Workers negotiate over money wages based on their expectation of the aggregate price level. Based on their expectation of the demand for their products, firms determine the level of employment. Workers and firms have to wait and see if their expectations are realized or falsified.

The actual price level will result from the interaction of supply and demand. Firms will offer what they produce assuming for simplicity that they do not carry inventories between production periods. Aggregate demand will depend on the levels of consumption and investment. There is nothing that guarantees that the level (and composition) of output demanded will coincide with the level (and composition) of supply. Windfall gains and losses ensues from the confrontation of supply and demand. In face of persistent windfall losses, producers may reduce the level of employment or negotiate a reduction in money wages.

Keynes did not emphasize the role of windfall events in explaining the possibility of unemployment or economic fluctuations. Indeed, he assumed that short-period expectations were continuously fulfilled. If producers correctly foresee a reduction in the desired level of demand, they could either reduce the level of employment or negotiate a reduction in money wages.

Keynes's static equilibrium in *The General Theory* was given by the level of employment associated with the level of aggregate demand as determined by long-period expectations of entrepreneurs, the supply of money, the propensity to consume out of income, the state of preference for liquidity, and the money-wage rate. The level of employment thus determined could well be such that workers would not find jobs at the prevailing wage, thus characterizing a situation of involuntary unemployment.

6.6. Sources of Fluctuations in Monetary Economies

In Keynes's scheme, the levels of employment and price and the rates of interest and real wages (the endogenous variables) fluctuate according to the effect of changes in the independent variables namely, long-period expectations of entrepreneurs, the supply of money, the propensity to consume out of income, the state of preference for liquidity, and the money-wage rate.

The more volatile of the independent variables are the state of liquidity preference and the long-term expectations of investors. Both affect the rate of investment that is seen as the more unstable component of aggregate demand. Keynes ascribed great importance to the uncertainty associated to decisions involving long intervals of time. Expectations about the future always have an imponderable element, which, to a certain extent, makes the decision slightly (or, depending on the circumstances, fairly) irrational.

In stable environments, a set of beliefs develop, and decision makers become more confident about their choices. The imponderable is still there, but they do not ascribe a lot of weight to it. This does not mean that they might not turn pessimistic about the economy, in which case their long-period expectations will lead them to reduce the level of investments with obvious effects on employment. There might be objective reasons for the pessimism (the international market for a certain product is becoming sluggish) or simply the spread of some pessimistic subjective view.

Unstable environments increase the weight attributed to the imponderable. It is time to be careful and avoid committing resources with illiquid assets that is when the demand for liquidity increases creating pressures on the rate of interest, and, thus, negative influence on investment and consumption.

Some prominent Keynesians like G.L.S. Shackle and Paul Davidson ascribe great importance to the volatility of investment as a result of changes in expectations and the instability of the environment. Indeed, they tend to see Keynes's main contribution to economics associated with the instability of expectations and investment. The volatility of the level of employment would then be the central concern of this strand of Keynesian thought.

6.7. The Persistence of Unemployment

If the instability of employment is undesirable, the persistence of it is even worse. Keynes had a very pessimistic view on the prospects of self-adjustment of market economies. He thought that the key adjusting variables (the interest rate and the money-wage rate) were slow to change; and when they changed, the economy did not respond in the right direction. In this respect Keynes was not an apologist of market economies, quite the contrary.

Keynes (VII, p. 14) thought that money wages were slow to fall in face of unemployment. His argument for the rigidity of wages was the following: "Since there is imperfect mobility of labour, and wages do not tend to an exact equality of net advantage in different occupations, any individual or group of individuals, who consent to a reduction of money-wages relatively to others, will suffer a *relative* reduction in real wages, which is a sufficient justification to resist it. . . . The effect of combination on the part of a group of workers is to protect their *relative* real wage."

However, if in face of acute unemployment, money wages start falling, the question still persists about the response of aggregate demand. Keynes saw a number of "pathological" responses, that is, responses that would lead to greater unemployment. The effects of changes in money wages on aggregate demand are well known, and we shall not endevor to list them all. Suffice it to quote a few of Keynes's (VII) most important remarks:

> If . . . we restrict our argument to the case of a closed system, and assume that there is nothing to be hoped, but if anything the contrary, form the repercussions of the new distribution of real incomes on the community's propensity to spend, it follows that we must base any hopes of favourable results to employment from a reduction in money-wages mainly on an improvement in investment due either to an increased marginal efficiency of capital . . . or a decreased rate of interest (pp. 264–265).

> The contingency, which is favourable to an increase in the marginal efficiency of capital, is that in which money-wages are believed to have touched bottom, so that further changes are expected to be in the upward direction. The most unfavourable contingency is that in which money-wages are slowly sagging downwards. . . . When we enter on a period of weakening effective demand, a sudden large reduction of money-wages to a level so low that no one believes in its indefinite continuance would be the event most favourable to a strengthening of effective demand. But this could only be accomplished by an administrative decree and is scarcely practical politics under a system of free wage-bargaining. (pp. 264–265).It is, therefore, on the effect of a falling wage- and price-level on the demand for money that those who believe in the serf-adjusting quality of the economic system must rest the weight of their argument (p. 266).

Keynes was doubtful about the efficacy of reducing money wages; and if the only effect that could really attenuate the persistence of unemployment was a reduction in the rate of interest, he favored an increase in money supply. However, even the reduction in the rate of interest was not sure because if the recession was associated with uncertain prospects about the future, agents would tend to absorb whatever amount of money the monetary authority decided to throw in the market.

Keynes's pessimism on the self-adjusting properties of market economies resulted from the rigidity of the money wage and interest rates, on the one hand, and on the ambiguity of effects associated with the fluidity of money wages.

6.8. ORTHODOX VERSUS HETERODOX VIEWS ON SELF-ADJUSTMENT

In macroeconomics textbooks, Keynesian theory is identified with the case of rigid money wages. This is, of course, an incorrect interpretation that results either from an incomplete reading of *The General Theory* or a partial interpretation of Keynes's ideas, which, for some reason, elects one of the two alternative (but not excludent) possibilities mentioned by Keynes. Another intriguing aspect of the current orthodox literature is the selection of effects of changes in money wages that unambiguously lead the economy to full employment. What is even more curious is the fact that in the literature itself one finds pathological effects (different from those mentioned in *The General Theory*) that the authors chose to ignore.

The bias toward a view that only privileges either wage rigidity or well-behaved effects, completely abandoning the pathological cases, can only result from a dogma, the dogma according to which market forces, in a competitive setting, work. Even if, from an empirical point of view, the perverse effects were irrelevant, the fact that they are theoretically sound should be sufficient to deserve notice.

In order to illustrate the dogmatic attitude of the orthodoxy, I introduce a semi-formal presentation of the determinants of aggregate demand, taking into account not only some of the effects discussed by Keynes but also others found in the literature. Consumption is usually seen as a function of disposable income (D), wealth (W) and the real rate of interest ($i - p$, where i is the nominal interest rate and p is the expected rate of inflation):

$$C = C(D, W, i - p),$$

where $D = Y - T - p[(M + B)] / P, W = (M + B)/P + K$,
Y = total income, T = taxes, P = price level, M = stock of money, B = stock of governemt bonds, and K = stock of physical capital.

The definition of disposable income is a simplified version of the definition given by Sargent (1979, p. 16): total income minus taxes minus "the perceived rate of capital loss on the real value of the public's net claims on the government." (The idea of the latter deduction from total income is that inflation imposes a tax on assets held by the public. The definition of wealth follows the conventional specification: the sum of the stocks of real outstanding financial and physical assets.)

Investment demand is usually seen as a function of the ratio of prospective returns measured in terms of the marginal efficiency of capital (Q) to the real interest rate:

$$I = I(q),$$

where $q = Q/(I-r)$.

Aggregate demand can thus be written as follows:

$$A = A\{Y - T - p[(M+B)/P], (M+B)/P, q, I-p\}. \quad (6.1)$$

In general, an asset market equilibrium equation of the following type is appended:

$$L(i, Y) = M/P.$$

Assuming a typical production function and perfect competition, it can be shown (see Sargent, 1979, p. 50) that

$$dP/P = dW/W - (F''/F'^2)\, dY, \quad (6.2)$$

where F' and F'' are the first and second derivatives of the production function that respect to labor.

In the typical Keynesian model, the aggregate demand function has all the arguments listed in equation **(6.1)**, and it can be shown that, given the money wage, the level of employment the level of aggregate demand may not be sufficient to employ all workers willing to work at the prevailing real wage. This is the conventional Keynesian static equilibrium result. If money wages fall, and thus through equation (6.2) the price level falls, given the anticipated rate of inflation (p), there will be an increase in real balances creating pressures for the interest rate to fall (Keynes effect). The reduction in the rate of interest tends to activate both investment and consumption. The increase in the price level also increases the value of wealth (Pigou effect) thus inducing greater consumption. These are the favorable effects for employment.

But there are adverse effects as well. The reduction in the price level increases the loss on the real value of the public's net claims on the government, thus reducing disposable income and consumption.[2] Deflationary expectations ($p < 0$) increase the expected real interest rate, thus inhibiting investment and consumption.[3]

Orthodox economists are optimistic (and apologetic of market economies): they believe that only the favorable effects prevail. That is why they privilege money wage flexibility and blame rigidity for the persistence of unemployment. Heterodox economists, on the other hand, are pessimistic about the prospects of self-adjustment through wage deflation and favor institutions that reduce the degree of wage flexibility.

As shown in **Figure 6.1**, the greater the predominance of favorable effects, the more desirable wage flexibility becomes. On the other hand, if there are reasons to believe that unfavorable effects might prevail, the best situation

FIGURE 6.1

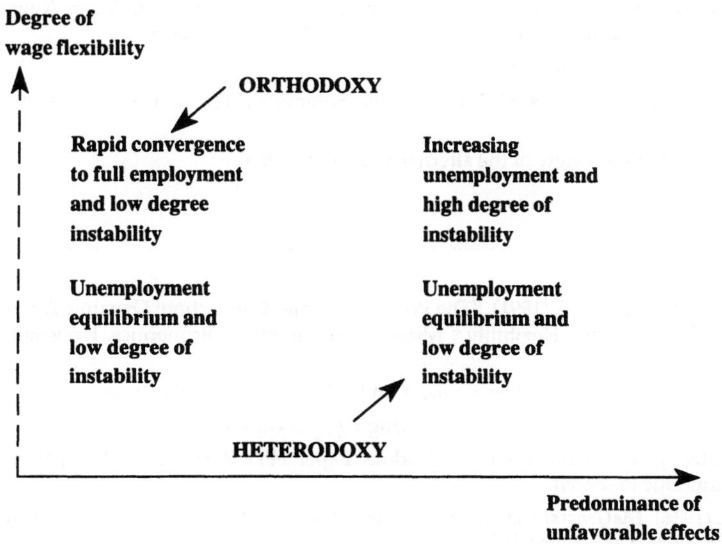

is one in which wages are rigid downwards. Keynes (VII, p. 269) himself was a heterodox: "It follows, therefore, that if labour were to respond to conditions of gradually diminishing employment by offering its services at a gradually diminishing money-wage, this would not, as a rule, have the effect of reducing real wages and might even have the effect of increasing them, through its adverse influence on the volume of output. The chief result of this policy would be to cause a great instability of prices, so violent perhaps as to make business calculations futile in an economic society functioning after the manner of that in which we live."

The reasons that led the profession to ascribe to *The General Theory* and Keynes the notion that unemployment resulted from rigid money wages are intriguing. Keynes did believe that wages were slow to fall, but his message was clearly that flexibility would not solve the problem. Keynesians are right in discussing explanatory hypotheses for the existence of wage rigidity,[4] but they do no good in disregarding the ambiguous results coming from flexibility. The preference for unambiguously favorable effects and, thus, the self-adjusting property of market economies can result only from a vision or an ideology about the functioning of capitalist economies. Logic alone will not do it.

NOTES

1. It is interesting to note that, judging from the point of view of *The General Theory*, Keynes's *Treatise on Money*, published in 1930, was itself a piece of orthodox theory.

2. This effect is found in Sargent (1979, p. 61).

3. This effect is found in Tobin (1975), Delong and Summers (1984) and Amadeo and Dutt (1991).

4. See Solow (1990) for a review of the alternative explanations.

REFERENCES

Amadeo, E. J., and Dutt, A. K. (1991). "The Wicksell-Keynes Connection: Dynamic Analysis, Loanable Funds, and Wage Flexibility," Mimeo, Department of Economics, University of Notre Dame, 1991.

Chick, V. (1983) *Macroeconomics after Keynes*. Cambridge, MA: The MIT Press.

Delong, J. B., and Summers, L. (1984) "The Changing Cyclical Variability of

Economic Activity in the United States," Working Paper 1450, Washington, D.C., National Bureau of Economic Research.

Keynes, J. M. (1936). *The General Theory of Employment, Money, and Interest*. London: Macmillan. Referred to in the text as Keynes, VII.

Keynes, J. M. (1973). *The Collected Writings of John Maynard Keynes*, Vol. XIII, *The General Theory and After*, edited by D. Moggridge. London: Macmillan, St. Martin's Press for the Royal Economic Society. Referred to in the text as JMK, XIII.

Sargent, T. (1979). *Macroeconomic Theory*, New York: Academic Press.

Solow, R. (1990). *The Labor Market as an Institution*, Cambridge: Basil Blackwell,.

Tobin, J. (1975). "Keynesian Models of Recession and Depression." *American Economic Review*, 65, pp. 195–202.

INDEX

MIX
Papier aus verantwortungsvollen Quellen
Paper from responsible sources
FSC® C105338

If you have any concerns about our products,
you can contact us on
ProductSafety@springernature.com

In case Publisher is established outside the EU,
the EU authorized representative is:
Springer Nature Customer Service Center GmbH
Europaplatz 3, 69115 Heidelberg, Germany

Printed by Libri Plureos GmbH
in Hamburg, Germany